LIVING IN THE TEXT

Living in the Text

Becoming People of the Book

JEFF VOTH *and* JESSE MULLER

WIPF & STOCK · Eugene, Oregon

LIVING IN THE TEXT
Becoming People of the Book

Copyright © 2025 Jeff Voth and Jesse Muller. All rights reserved. Except for brief quotations in critical publications or reviews, no part of this book may be reproduced in any manner without prior written permission from the publisher. Write: Permissions, Wipf and Stock Publishers, 199 W. 8th Ave., Suite 3, Eugene, OR 97401.

Wipf & Stock
An Imprint of Wipf and Stock Publishers
199 W. 8th Ave., Suite 3
Eugene, OR 97401

www.wipfandstock.com

PAPERBACK ISBN: 979-8-3852-0103-7
HARDCOVER ISBN: 979-8-3852-0104-4
EBOOK ISBN: 979-8-3852-0105-1

Unless otherwise indicated, Scriptures taken from the Holy Bible, New International Version®, NIV®. Copyright © 1973, 1978, 1984, 2011 by Biblica, Inc.™ Used by permission of Zondervan. All rights reserved.

Scripture quotations marked ESV are from The Holy Bible, English Standard Version®, © 2001 by Crossway, a publishing ministry of Good News Publishers. Used by permission. All rights reserved.

Scripture quotations marked NRSV are from the New Revised Standard Version Bible, copyright © 1989 National Council of the Churches of Christ in the United States of America. Used by permission. All rights reserved worldwide.

To the One who has infused the text with His everlasting life.

Table of Contents

Acknowledgments ix

Introduction xi

PART I: *Why We Need to Live in the Text*

Chapter 1: The Bible Is Needed 3

Chapter 2: The Bible Is Ignored 13

Chapter 3: The Bible Is Communal 22

PART II: *Living Out the Text*

Chapter 4: HIStory Revealed 35

Chapter 5: Jeff's Story 49

Chapter 6: Jesse's Story 60

PART III: *How to Live in the Text*

Chapter 7: The Bible Sown 73

Chapter 8: The Bible Buried 83

Chapter 9: The Bible Harvest 93

Bibliography 101

Acknowledgments

LIVING IN THE TEXT is not just the title of this book, it is the lifestyle of our church, Church 3434. We are grateful to our church family for learning, growing, and embodying this ancient and new culture centered on the Word. We are honored to do life alongside such encouraging and loving brothers and sisters. It is a gift to struggle well with this community, living out the hope, light, and life of Christ together.

We also would not be the men we are without the love, friendship, and encouragement of our amazing wives, Lori Voth and Hannah Muller. You help us be all Christ made us to be.

Introduction

THIS IS A MESSAGE of hope, not because of where we are but because of what could be. The world is loud, and our hearts and minds match the pace we observe in the world around us. We claim that the Lord is our Shepherd, yet we rarely experience the peaceful streams of his presence. Society, bolstered by the study of our minds and attention spans, is specially equipped to stimulate and draw us in. Constantly. We, as a people, are addicted to entertainment. Our hands and minds are perpetually in motion from distraction to distraction as the world tells us that our desires and impulses must be obeyed. For those of us who follow the crucified Savior, an intimidating challenge faces our faith unlike most generations before: we are consumers. The Western world is largely designed to please and encourage immediate gratification of desires. It is in this context of stimulation, innovation, and the desire for more that our faith is to be built. In contrast to all the noise, the foundation of Christianity is a simple book.

Now we do not use the term "simple book" in a negative way, as the Bible is a complex, masterful literary work that spans centuries. It is simply quieter than most of the things with which we interact. Nor are we ignoring the fact that Christianity is firmly rooted in the identity and salvation found only in Jesus Christ. But the authority of Christianity flows directly from what we know of this book, or collection of books. A significant challenge that the Western church faces in our day is the vast difference in values between the church and the world. Our environment affirms that this life is about my desires, and that I deserve those desires be fulfilled immediately. The Bible tells me that this existence is about Christ, and following him means sacrificially denying myself. Growth in him is a gradual, daily process that we never totally achieve. See the difference?

Our fear, which we have seen and experienced personally, is that our perception of society has bled into our pursuit of Christ. We neglect the "mundane" and "ordinary" disciplines, such as Bible study and prayer, in favor of quick spiritual highs, easy one-liners, feel-good messages, and a steady stream of podcasts and videos. We want the results of time with God without the work. The core of this issue is our perception and treatment of God's word. If this book truly is the revealed story of God's interaction with humanity and his plan for our lives in him, it deserves more than a weekly glance on a Sunday. It deserves more than a surface level reference that sounds great but ignores context. It deserves our full attention, reverence, and faithfulness as we follow Christ.

We are part of something bigger than ourselves. We are part of the church, the bride of Christ. This thing isn't about any one of us, but about Christ in us and in the world. If Jesus is the Way, the Truth, and the Life, what happens if we don't know the way he opened for us, the truth he taught, or the life he lived? What happens when we claim Christianity yet ignore the text that tells us what that term actually means?

We need to return to our foundation, which is why we wrote this book: to show the need for communal interaction with the Bible and offer practical steps for believers of all backgrounds to prioritize God's word in their communities. This book does not only ask "How can I grow in God's word?" but "How can we grow in God's word together?" The world needs Christians who can answer that question, who live in Christ and his word. It's time to live in the text.

PART I
Why We Need to Live in the Text

> Blessed is the one who does not walk in step with the wicked or stand in the way that sinners take or sit in the company of mockers, but whose delight is in the law of the Lord, and who meditates on his law day and night. That person is like a tree planted by streams of water, which yields its fruit in season and whose leaf does not wither—whatever they do prospers. —Psalm 1:1–3

> With our civilisation facing multiplying existential challenges, how quickly stagnation and decline could become a freefall. You don't need an overactive imagination to ponder the brutal possible consequences, especially if progressive politicians fail to offer compelling answers. Our lives are shortening, our wellbeing is falling, our security being dismantled. These are the conditions of despair, and a bitter harvest beckons. —Owen Jones[1]

When comparing the promise of prosperity in Ps 1:1–3 with the apparent demise of Western civilization alluded to in the above quote, what is the community of faith to do? What is an

---

1. Jones, "Politicians Are Right."

Part I: Why We Need To Live In The Text

individual who lives in the community of faith to do? Fortunately, this predicament is not new, and our brothers and sisters in the faith have effectively and successfully weathered these despair-laden storms for millennia. One would expect that if the Ps 1 promise of prosperity is true, even in the midst of cultural collapse, there should be some sort of model to follow—a pattern to emulate as a template. That is where living in the text comes in.

In this section, we will discuss why the Bible is needed, how it is ignored, and how it is a communal book. Those who call on the name of Jesus have been chosen to be the representatives of his kingdom. This kingdom does not work like the kingdoms of the world. If Christ followers are to accurately and fully represent Jesus in the world, we must remain grounded in his word, the Bible. His text—his plan—his life.

1

The Bible Is Needed

Take up and read. —St. Augustine[1]

"SCROLL ME!"

ON A DAILY BASIS, every one of us is inundated with innumerable words and images. We are beckoned to endlessly scroll or click on a cell phone, computer, or other device. Images scream at us: "Look at me!" "Click on me!" "Read me!" "Respond to me!" "Like me!" The vessel of our minds is launched into a sea of words, pictures, and images vying for our attention. Have you ever wondered about the effects? What does this often aimless, misdirected voyage do to our minds? This voyage has only been expanded by technology and media progress, producing features such as the infinite scroll. Infinite scroll:

- "[Is] a feature that allows us to continuously scroll down a page, removing any need to press 'refresh' or hit a 'next page' button."
- Can be "likened to a virtual slot machine—which offers dopamine-inducing variable rewards, thereby making it hyper-addictive."

---

1. Augustine, *Confessions*, 186.

- "Can overwhelm users with a constant stream of information, which can lead to feelings of stress, anxiety, and fatigue."[2]

The above term points to a staggering bottom line: through repeated, mindless use, words can often lose, or have their meanings distorted. It's called familiarity. When one becomes familiar with something, he or she becomes so used to it, or numbed by repeated, mindless exposure to it, that it's like it's not even there anymore. The intellectual struggle or conflict has been bypassed, unwittingly affecting the entire being like anesthesia before surgery—surgery being done on one's heart, yet with eyes wide open. Jesus was referring to this phenomenon when he said,

> The eye is the lamp of the body. If your eyes are healthy, your whole body will be full of light. But if your eyes are unhealthy, your whole body will be full of darkness. If then the light within you is darkness, how great is that darkness! (Matt 6:22–23)

The psalmist affirms this theme repeatedly:

> The precepts of the LORD are right, giving joy to the heart. The commands of the LORD are radiant, giving light to the eyes. (Ps 19:8)

> My eyes are ever on the LORD, for only he will release my feet from the snare. (Ps 25:8)

The writer of Proverbs adds another level of understanding to the potential effects upon a person's soul as images enter him via not only the doorway of his eyes, but the ears as well.

> Light in a messenger's eyes brings joy to the heart, and good news gives health to the bones. (Prov 15:30)

> Ears that hear and eyes that see—the LORD has made them both. (Prov 20:12)

Bottom line: what goes through the doors of our eyes or ears permeates into our minds and affects our whole being. One should pay much attention to what enters his or her head through the eyes

2. Hilotin, "Deadly Scroll."

and ears. Legendary theologian and preacher Charles Spurgeon once said,

> The mind can descend far lower than the body, for in it there are bottomless pits. The flesh can bear only a certain number of wounds and no more, but the soul can bleed in ten thousand ways, and die over and over again each hour.[3]

"SCROLL ME NOW!"

While the effects of the internet and the amounts of images available to us at this point in history have certainly compounded and expedited the dulling effects of familiarity that come from the infinite scroll, it's not a new thing. St. Augustine of Hippo in the fourth century was a pre-internet troller and scroller. He would recount in his tell-all classic entitled *Confessions* how he was, at one point in his life, a man who would attend what were known as "peep shows" and literally scroll and troll through real, live images of scantily clad and naked women on a regular basis. He was also drawn to all of the latest thoughts of the day, ultimately landing on a philosophy that taught that what one did to one's body had no lasting, eternal effects on him as a person. This eventual doctor of the church and potentially one of, if not the, most famous of the church fathers, was essentially a fourth-century porn addict who would eventually enter a sexual relationship with a woman outside of marriage, fathering an illegitimate son.

It sounds like this could and has happened in the current cultural setting as well, doesn't it? It seems that we read almost daily about a famous pastor or ministry leader that has done the same things as Augustine confessed. However, one day, while alone in a garden, Augustine was beckoned by the voice of what sounded like a young child in Latin to "Tolle lege; Tolle lege," or "Take up and read; Take up and read" in English. He did just that and the rest is church history. He picked up that sacred scroll, the Bible,

---

3. Spurgeon, "Honey in the Mouth," 485.

Part I: Why We Need To Live In The Text

and began to gaze at it intently. Here is his own version of that life-altering experience with God, the voice, and the scroll:

> So was I speaking and weeping in the most bitter contrition of my heart, when, lo! I heard from a neighbouring house a voice, as of boy or girl, I know not, chanting, and oft repeating, "Take up and read; Take up and read." Instantly, my countenance altered, I began to think most intently whether children were wont in any kind of play to sing such words: nor could I remember ever to have heard the like. So checking the torrent of my tears, I arose; interpreting it to be no other than a command from God to open up the book, and read the first chapter I should find.[4]

Whether it was an actual child calling to Augustine, an angelic host, or a voice from the book itself, this amazing man was sucked into the vortex that is the living word of God—the Bible. He took it up and was caught. The scroll was opened to Rom 13:13–14, where he read the following words:

> Let us behave decently, as in the daytime, not in carousing and drunkenness, not in sexual immorality and debauchery, not in dissension and jealousy. Rather, clothe yourselves with the Lord Jesus Christ, and do not think about how to gratify the desires of the flesh.

As the living word is apt to do, it cut him to his core. Then, under the guidance of the Holy Spirit himself, that word burned through the muck of death that had seeped in on Augustine and made a way for this formerly arrogant, now convicted man to repent. Captivated by the surgical precision of God's word, Augustine began to scroll through the text of Scripture in a new way and with a fresh passion. Healthy scrolling through the living word of God brought an end to the unhealthy trolling habits that led to unhealthy and potentially deadly results. His brilliant and quick mind, now being rejuvenated and renewed by the living word, would ultimately be used by God to define, expound upon, and

---

4. Augustine, *Confessions*, 186.

communicate some of the most important concepts and doctrines of the Christian faith: grace, faith, sin, evil, the Trinity, and countless other vitally important subjects. Thanks be to God that Augustine took the Bible up, read it, and became a person who lived in the text.

TIMELESS, LIFE-GIVING SCROLLS

The scroll, or book of the Bible that Augustine opened, called the book of Romans, was really part of the ancient collective story of Israel in a New Testament context. We mean by this that the New Testament is a set of twenty-seven books that build upon the story of God's people, which is told in the thirty-nine books of the Old Testament, and spans from the dawn of time until about 400 BC. His people, the Israelites, would endure blessings, curses, enslavement, and freedom, along with thousands of years repeating this cycle. However, God, in his grace, would always provide them with a word—words that would come through prophets, priests, and kings—some good, some bad, some indifferent. These words would ultimately be collected, recited, remembered, forgotten, and re-remembered. Regardless of the cultural circumstance, the unchanging God of creation would continue to reach for his people, calling them to himself, speaking to them—always reaffirming his loving concern through his powerful and changeless word, ultimately culminating in the life, death, and resurrection of Jesus.

One such instance occurred between the early fifth and late fourth centuries BC. God reached for his people in the midst of confusing and depressing times. It is recounted in the biblical books of Ezra and Nehemiah, which were initially written as one scroll. The main characters in these books are Ezra, an influential scribe and priest, and Nehemiah, governor and "cupbearer" to the pagan, yet benevolent King Artaxerxes I. The two men lived as captives in Babylon, but, because of their high-ranking status, were allowed to join their countrymen in the partially repopulated Palestine. However, despite the fact that the temple in Jerusalem had been victoriously rebuilt, the small Jewish community that lived there struggled in fear and feelings of defenselessness at the hands of their non-Jewish, aggressive neighbors.

God's people needed to re-find their identity in the Lord and return to his word. At times, they were successful. At other times, they were not. It is our sincere hope that the plights, victories, and hard learned lessons of the people in Ezra and Nehemiah will be plights, victories, and lessons from which we, as God's people today, will learn. We will learn together that although these people experienced these things thousands of years ago, we endure the same things. God's truth is timeless—subject to neither time, nor culture.

WHAT ABOUT YOU? WHAT ABOUT TODAY?

The two questions above are imperative—vitally important for the people of God to answer if we are going to do more than merely survive. We believe that we are to thrive and create vibrant and reverberating families and churches that literally transform the communities where they are located. So . . .

What about you?

What about today?

You may have read the title of this chapter and concluded that it is a really good idea to read the Bible—that it is a healthy activity. It could be that you feel you should read the Bible, just like you should exercise, brush your teeth, save your money, and call your family more often. These are all things that you know should be a part of your normal life, but you respond to them to deal with that nagging guilt in the back of your mind, the little voice that says if you go too long without doing them, you will feel bad about yourself. So, you do them.

However, we are saying that living in the text is about much more than this, more than dealing with guilt or setting another resolution. We want you to see that interacting with the Bible through God's Spirit is more like the taking of your next breath and having a consistent source of food and water in order to sustain that breath, regardless of the circumstances that come your way.

We need God's word. We *need* it. We often use the word "need" needlessly. Very few things do we actually need. Scripture is the revealed story of God at work in the world. It's the communication of his salvation and relationship with creation. Jesus, our Lord and example, continually quoted the word in his teachings and prayers. The whole of the Bible is inspired by God's Spirit and is useful for teaching, rebuking, correcting, and training in righteousness (2 Tim 2:16-17). We can't overstress how vital it is for life in Jesus.

So, how do you view the Bible? Give some thought to the following questions.

Do you use the Bible as décor?

A person who uses it in this fashion says, "I believe in God and know that the Bible is important because it is his word. In fact, I own several copies, and they are in visible locations in my home collecting dust. I don't really 'read' it beyond Sundays when it is on the screen at church, or every so often when the dust is removed from those on display in my home—especially on deep cleaning days and/or major holidays."

Do you use the Bible as a safety net?

A person who uses it in this fashion says, "The Bible makes me feel better when I am having a hard time in life. There are certain passages I return to when I am struggling emotionally. I know God loves me and is there for me, and I know he will speak to me through his word on my darkest days, but when life is good, I must admit that it usually goes back on the shelf until my next breakdown and/or the next holiday comes around."

Part I: Why We Need To Live In The Text

Do you use the Bible as a hammer?

A person who uses it in this fashion says, "There are so many wrong opinions in the world, and God's truth is the best way to respond to them and the people who hold to them. I am absolutely sure that I know exactly how to respond, and I must smash those who don't, especially if a person doesn't know or follow Jesus. God's commands must be shared to expose deceit and reveal the truth. I care more about the truth in the immediate circumstance instead of anyone's feelings. I must use the Bible to pound anyone, any place, or any time into truthfulness."

Do you use the Bible as a life-giving manual?

A person who uses it in this fashion says, "The Bible is God's inspired truth and must be studied to know right from wrong. I know that it has the answers to any and every controversial subject and theological question and, with enough prayerful searching and support from like-minded brothers and sisters, I can find answers to all of life's questions. Yes, there will be messy, difficult, and trying times, but in the Bible, I will find what I need to know to live the best life morally, politically, financially, and spiritually. As for me and my family, we will choose to live in the text and use it as our all-purpose, every-purpose, any-purpose manual."

While it may be true that there are parts of the above examples that you agree or disagree with, the important question to ask is, why was the Bible written? Or, what is its purpose? Do you know the answer?

It's to know the thesis—Jesus.

Very simply, it's to know the good news of Jesus Christ. To do so, we must live in and through his life alongside a community of brothers and sisters. God uses his word to shape every area of our lives: the mundane, special, joyful, tragic, and everything in between. Instead of an infinite scroll through powerless and finite images, it must be a purposeful scroll through the infinitely valuable scroll that is the Bible. We need the word. We walk blind without it, leaving God's foundation of truth. By the Holy Spirit, it is a guide for life, a weapon against sin and death, and the revelation of God himself. Let's live in the text with the One who is the thesis of it.

SUMMARY POINTS

- "Infinite scroll" is a modern function that automatically refreshes websites to provide viewers with new content continually. Studies have shown that this type of scrolling floods viewers with information and stimulation, numbing and addicting with the promise of dopamine highs.

- "Scrolling" is not a new concept. Jesus, David, and Solomon all referenced the impact of sights and sounds. What our eyes and ears consume affects the entirety of our person: mind, body, and soul.

- Saint Augustine of Hippo, the original "troller and scroller," was trapped in sinful passions and lusts, particularly in his habit of objectifying women. God brought him freedom through the word, particularly through the book of Romans. Augustine went on to be a history-making church leader and thinker.

- The Old and the New Testaments of the Bible tell God's story. He chose a people for himself, the Israelites, to reveal his love and salvation. Through trials and tribulations, God always reached out to them with his word, culminating in the life, death, and resurrection of Jesus.

- Interacting with the Bible is more than a part of your daily routine, like brushing your teeth. Reading the Bible is more akin to basic survival needs such as breathing, drinking, eating, and securing shelter.

- We need the Bible because it is God's revelation of himself and his salvation. Jesus, our example, continually quoted Scripture in his teachings and prayers. The entirety of the

Bible is inspired by God's Spirit. It's not just another good book to read.

- Four common perceptions of the Bible include:

   a) *Décor:* Bibles are decorations set up for appearances in the home, but not used apart from Sundays or special events.

   b) *Safety Net:* Scripture is a secure place to turn when facing difficulty, but it's quickly forgotten when things are going well.

   c) *Hammer:* The Bible is a tool to correct and instruct, a weapon against those who are wrong. The desire for truth overshadows the need for love.

   d) *Life-Giving Manual:* The Bible is a guide for all of life. Through prayer and community, you can find instruction for how to live and what to believe.

- Though there are elements of truth in each of these, the ultimate point of the Bible is to know Jesus. Living in the text begins and ends with him. The truth found in these other views flows out of a relationship with him.

2

The Bible Is Ignored

THE NICKNAME GAME

How often are we surrounded with near-constant stimulation, even when we do not intentionally choose it? This noise attempts to continually entertain and influence our hearts and minds through screens, voices, and advertisements. Although not every noise is harmful in and of itself, the outcome of being around so much stimulation can be. We get so used to sights and sounds that something feels off in the quiet. We get restless and fidgety. It's the feeling of sitting with a group in awkward silence. You cringe internally (or externally), counting the seconds until you can leave, hoping something interesting will happen. We train ourselves to crave something. *Anything.* Anything but the peace we need. For most of us, technology relieves the discomfort like white noise: constant, consistent, hypnotic, and, ultimately, empty. This noise, and the need for it, erodes our ability to listen to, process, and follow God's voice in our lives.

It reminds me of an exercise in college. I (Jesse) was going through a training week to prepare for a mission trip to Greece, and every day was filled with team building activities, cross-cultural exercises, and services. One game that we played was all about finding a partner blindfolded. Forty people were divided into pairs and set on two sides of a room. Each person was given a nickname, and partners had to yell out each other's names to find

Part I: Why We Need To Live In The Text

one another. (They were simple names like apple, spring, airplane, etc.) As you can imagine, forty blindfolded people screaming out random objects as they stumbled into each other was chaotic, inefficient, and comical. In an effort to be heard over the noise, everyone yelled louder. It didn't exactly help. Among the forty voices screaming (including my own), only one was meant for me. Even my own shouting hurt my chances of hearing my partner.

This is how many Christians live their lives.

God has given us his revealed word, the Bible, that is alive and active (Heb 4:12). It teaches us about his character, his actions, and his salvation (2 Tim 3:14–17). It is described as food (Deut 8:3), a weapon (Eph 6:17), and a standard for life (Jas 1:23–24). God speaks through his word. It is a voice meant for us. But it's not the only voice speaking.

How much time do you spend on a screen in a day? Now, we know that a majority of people require a screen to complete their work. Those emails won't send themselves. But have you ever stopped to think about where your attention goes in a day? For many Americans, social media is a regular staple. We found several statistics, but the most telling are from Pew Research. Here is the percentage of Americans who used various social media as of 2024: YouTube, 83 percent; Facebook, 68 percent; Instagram, 47 percent; Pinterest, 35 percent; TikTok, 33 percent.[1]

This book isn't specifically a critique of social media, but it is a challenge to consider how we spend our time. Each statistic is a different voice that molds our minds and spirits. Regardless of what we interact with online, each medium trains us to seek quick stimulation. We scroll past anything that doesn't catch our attention in two seconds. How often do we numbly pass post after post, video after video? We lose focus, floating from one voice to the next as the minutes and hours pass.

The danger isn't just *what* we see and hear. It's also about *how*. There is an article titled "Is Google Making Us Ungodly?" by Samuel James. You may have a similar reaction to the title as we did: "Well, of course! Do you know how much messed up stuff is

---

1. Gottfried, "Americans' Social Media Use."

on the internet? It's basically instant-access sin." While often true, that isn't what James wrote about. Instead, the article deals with *how* we interact with the internet and Scripture. Is the way we approach the internet the way we should approach the Bible, jumping through dozens of ideas, pictures, and videos in one sitting? No, it's not. Our brains get used to switching from one post or page to another, constantly moving. We're told the Bible deserves a different kind of attention: a dedicated, gradual, lifelong living in the text. We are to slowly consider what God teaches as we depend on him for guidance.[2]

But do Christians treat the word as it deserves? Compare the social media stats above to the average time Christians spend in the Bible: 45 percent of Christians read the Bible weekly, 12 percent read it once or twice a month, 9 percent read it several times a year, 33 percent seldom or never read it, and 1 percent didn't know.[3]

The most disciplined statistic for Christians began at the weekly mark. A majority of Americans access a social media platform daily. Beyond this, the average screen time for Americans as of 2024 was seven hours and three minutes a day.[4] Some of that is necessary for work and productivity, but see the comparison? Or, what about children? This is from a 2018 article by the Centers for Disease Control and Prevention:

> According to the Kaiser Family Foundation, kids ages 8–18 now spend, on average, a whopping 7.5 hours in front of a screen for entertainment each day, 4.5 of which are spent watching TV. Over a year, that adds up to 114 full days watching a screen for fun. That's just the time they spend in front of a screen for entertainment. It doesn't include the time they spend on the computer at school for educational purposes or at home for homework.[5]

---

2. James, "Is Google Making Us Ungodly?"
3. Pew Research Center, "Frequency of Reading Scripture."
4. Howarth, "Alarming Average Screen Time."
5. Centers for Disease Control, "Screen Time vs. Lean Time."

Part I: Why We Need To Live In The Text

We are not saying that every person must spend an hour in the Bible every day to be a "good Christian," nor are we saying that screens are the devil and need to be burned in the streets. But we should consider where our attention is going. What voice are we seeking? We're playing the nickname game, but we're not even listening.

THEY FORGOT THE LAW OF THE LORD

Israel stopped listening. Even though God had delivered them from Egypt, brought them to the promised land, and established their nation, they forgot his voice. Anytime you are reading the Bible and see a phrase along the lines of "They forgot the law of the LORD," just know things are about to get bad. Forgetting equals disobedience. Israel listened to other voices that sounded reasonable. Some spoke of other gods to serve, some encouraged political alliances for power, and others highlighted shady financial opportunities. God's law was ignored. One telling statement comes from Judg 21:25 (ESV): "Everyone did what was right in his own eyes."

Israel's rebellion kept building, and judgment came. The Babylonians, the big, bad power of the day, came and burned everything down in 586 BC because the people had turned away from God. Jerusalem was destroyed and the temple was torn down. Ignoring God's word has consequences.

Several generations later, Jews were allowed to return to Jerusalem. This is where we begin the story of Ezra and Nehemiah that we reviewed in the first chapter. Exiles had begun to resettle the ruins and there was work to do. Beyond the physical rebuilding, the people needed a spiritual foundation again. The people needed to be reminded of the word.

THE WORD OR THE OPINION?

It is vital for the word to inform our values, though, sadly, Christians throughout history often allowed their values to inform the

The Bible Is Ignored

word. We make God in our image. For example, Germany was in an uncertain place in the early 1900s. World War I caused death and destruction across Europe from 1914 to 1918. Millions died, and the world was in an uneasy peace in its aftermath. In 1919, Germany signed the Treaty of Versailles to end the Great War. This document placed the blame for the war completely on Germany and leveled harsh punishments on the people:

- 10 percent of Germany was given to the surrounding countries.
- All German colonies in China, the Pacific, and Africa were distributed to other powers.
- The German military was limited to 100,000 men.
- Germany couldn't produce specific military resources like tanks, armored cars, submarines, airplanes, and poison gas.
- Germany was required to repay $33 billion to the other nations involved in the war.[6]

These terms were much harsher than those President Woodrow Wilson initially offered in the Fourteen Points. The value of German money plummeted, so much so that there are pictures of Germans using bills as wallpaper.[7] It was worth more that way. They were crushed politically, financially, and socially.

Can you imagine how difficult it must have been to be a German at the time? Your entire nation was punished for a devastating war, your economy was decimated with the consequences, your military was largely disbanded, and you were the object of shame to the world. The people looked for hope and found it in the rising Nazi party. The Nazis proclaimed a chance for strength, honor, and pride. And they gained followers.

It was a slow fade to Nazi power, and their influence affected every area of life, much more than we have the space to interact with here adequately. However, one important group that faced

---

6. *Encyclopaedia Britannica*, "Treaty of Versailles."
7. United States Holocaust Museum, "Weimar Germany Reichsbanknote."

Part I: Why We Need To Live In The Text

the challenge of the new government was the church. A strong Christian tradition came face to face with the worldview of its day.

At first, Hitler looked like a good Christian. At least, that is how he wanted to appear. He proclaimed that Jesus was the "greatest Aryan hero"[8] (Aryan was the term used to describe the true super race of pure Germans. Jews were the opposite of this). Jesus' identity was just one foundational part of Christianity that the Nazi-influenced church attempted to change. Among others:

- The German National Church sought to cease the publication and dissemination of the Bible, replace the Bible with *Mein Kampf* in churches, remove all crucifixes and saints from churches, and replace all crosses with swastikas.[9]
- German Christians completely removed the Old Testament because of its Jewish influence, and some went further to deny the whole Bible.[10]
- German Christians taught that baptism was the act of joining the community of the nation. Communion was partaking in the "body of the earth that, firm and strong, remains true to German soil," and the wine was "the blood of the earth."[11]

These "Christians" saw the Bible through their beliefs rather than their beliefs through the Bible. We should begin our perspectives in Scripture, not seek to justify our formed opinions in the word. "German" came before "Christian," and followers of Christ became followers of the Nazi Party. Like strychnine in rat poison, Christians swallowed death because most of the message felt good. It was subtle (and not so subtle) changes that dismantled Christianity.

However, many opposed this shift within Germany. Believers who held to historic Christianity were known as the Confessing Church. One major leader and author of this time was a man

---

8. Metaxas, *Bonhoeffer*, 168.
9. Metaxas, *Bonhoeffer*, 171.
10. Metaxas, *Bonhoeffer*, 172.
11. Metaxas, *Bonhoeffer*, 173.

named Dietrich Bonhoeffer. This German pastor opposed the compromise in several ways. In his essay "The Church and the Jewish Question" he argued that the church was called to confront evils in government, assist all those persecuted by injustices, and "put a spoke in the wheel" of evil systems if more action was needed.[12] Bonhoeffer was sadly in the vast minority of church leaders. Far more allowed the political power of the day to inform their faith.

These were negative voices, but what do you do with "good" voices that aren't best? There are countless ministries, organizations, preachers, celebrities, and influencers who create videos, podcasts, television shows, and radio stations that offer helpful and encouraging content. We can't tell you the number of daily and weekly devotionals we have in our offices and email inboxes. There is a lot of good out there, but what if it removes our desire to be with Jesus personally?

The danger of having a continuous stream of teaching, preaching, and worship is that we equate interacting with content with being with Jesus. Although these can coexist, these sources are not supposed to be our foundation. You will be unhealthy if all you eat are vitamins and protein powder. Those aren't substantial enough to sustain you as you were designed to be. The same can be said for these secondary sources. They are great additions to our spiritual lives, but they should not form the totality of our spiritual lives. Hearing a convicting message, powerful worship song, or enlightening podcast cannot replace dedicated, intentional time with our Lord in prayer and study. Our relationship and life are with Jesus, not our favorite speaker, teacher, or leader.

We need the Bible. It is God's revealed word. Things go badly when we neglect it because there are so many other voices in the world, positive and negative. Our lens is so easily clouded. We need to be tethered to God's word and his Spirit as we follow his Son. Bible study is not just another "good thing to do." When we forget the Bible, we forget our Lord. A Harvard study stated that there

---

12. Holocaust Encyclopedia, "Dietrich Bonhoeffer."

PART I: WHY WE NEED TO LIVE IN THE TEXT

are over three hundred thousand modes of communication.[13] How many of those are drawing us closer to Jesus? How many are drowning out his voice?

SUMMARY POINTS

- We are surrounded with near-constant stimulation between screens, sights, and sounds. This stimulation can negatively affect our ability to hear God's voice, making it difficult for us to embrace silence and stillness.

- As of 2024, Americans used the following social media platforms: YouTube, 83 percent; Facebook, 68 percent; Instagram, 47 percent; Pinterest, 35 percent; TikTok, 33 percent.[14] Americans also spend an average of seven hours and three minutes a day on a screen.[15]

- Social media and the internet are not inherently evil, but it is worth taking note of how we are spending our time. Beyond what we access and the length of time we use these sources, our brains are also impacted by how we interact with the internet: scrolling from idea to idea, image to image, video to video in one sitting. This type of scrolling wires our brains to look for continual stimulation and activity.

- In comparison, we are to approach the Bible slowly in study, prayer, and reflection. That approach is undermined when our brains are trained to move through dozens of unique stimuli in one sitting.

- As of 2018, 45 percent of Christians read the Bible weekly, 12 percent read it once or twice a month, 9 percent read it several times a year, 33 percent seldom or never read it, and 1 percent didn't know.[16]

13. Hansel, *When I Relax I Feel Guilty*, 51–52.
14. Gottfried, "Americans' Social Media Use."
15. Howarth, "Alarming Average Screen Time."
16. Pew Research Center, "Frequency of Reading Scripture."

- "Success" is not simply being in the Bible every day, but prayerfully considering where our time and attention are going.
- Historically, when God's people ignored and forgot the law of God, bad things happened. When the Israelites forgot the One who delivered them from Egypt, Jerusalem was destroyed and the Temple was torn down.
- The story of Ezra and Nehemiah took place several generations later when the exiled Jews returned to Jerusalem to rebuild their physical and spiritual foundations by living in the word of God.
- Other voices seek to distract us from God's word. For Nazi Germany, political beliefs and nationalism informed spiritual beliefs rather than vice versa. These harmful voices from the culture infiltrated the church. An author, major leader, and German pastor in the 1930s and 1940s, Dietrich Bonhoeffer, opposed the change, along with a group called the Confessing Church. They held to Jesus and his truth.
- Positive voices can also make us ignore God. When we assume that "good" things like teachings, worship, podcasts, and videos equate to spending time with Jesus, we neglect personal time with him and his word.

3

The Bible Is Communal

If you want to go fast, go alone. If you want to go far, go together. —Unknown

I am because we are; and since we are, therefore I am.
—John S. Mbiti[1]

LIVING IN THE CONTEXT

It is important to know the context of something in order to understand it. The author's identity, intended audience, date, location, culture, and surrounding circumstances all impact the meaning of a written work. There is a vast difference between reading a newspaper from the 1800s, graffiti in your local town that is twenty years old, and a text message you just received from your friend. You can't approach these the same way. They aren't all for or to you, but you can learn something from all of them. We often read the Bible like it was written *to* us rather than *for* us. There is a big difference.

Did you know that only three of the sixty-six books in the Bible were written to individuals? First Timothy, 2 Timothy, and

---

1. Mbiti, *African Religions and Philosophy*, 106.

The Bible Is Communal

Titus. Every other book was written either to a group (like a letter) or for a group (like a historical record or poetry). Also, did you know that the vast majority of Christians only heard the Bible read aloud in a group setting for the first 1500 years of church history because they didn't have their own copy? Jews practiced similar group readings for centuries before that, too. Much of the Old and New Testaments were designed to be memorable because they were communicated orally. Interaction with the text was communal, and people then considered the teachings personally in light of the communal reading. The Bible is designed to be approached and studied *together*.

For many of us who have been members of the Western church, emphasis is given on our own devotional or quiet time. The regular, solitary practice of reading the Bible and praying is prioritized and taught as one of the greatest ways to grow spiritually. Start every morning with that cup of coffee, journal, and soft instrumental music as you crack open your Bible. Yet, we have to ask the question: Is this the only way God's word is meant to be read? Are we missing something?

We ask these questions to challenge our cultural lens as members of an individualistic society. One can go too far on either side of the spectrum, but we believe that many Christians have neglected the foundation of community when it comes to God's word. Studying and praying in private are great disciplines that we should commit ourselves to, but we should not isolate ourselves from brothers and sisters.

One of my favorite quotes on this idea is from Brad Harper and Paul Metzger. In their book, *Exploring Ecclesiology* ("Ecclesiology" meaning the study of the church), they write: "While relationship with Jesus is truly personal, it is by no means private, individualistic, and consumerist. It is public and interpersonal or communal."[2]

Public and interpersonal. The presence of these does not mean the absence of personal. If we truly desire to live in the text, it must be with others. You *can* follow Jesus by yourself, but it's not

---

2. Harper and Metzger, *Exploring Ecclesiology*, 41.

Part I: Why We Need To Live In The Text

biblical to try. There are several reasons why approaching the Bible in community is helpful.

Learning: Studying the Word

Very practically, we learn better with others. Biblical community positively influences our grasp of God's word through accountability and interaction. Accountability is a covering of protection and encouragement, not to mention healthy discomfort. I (Jesse) experienced this firsthand when a buddy of mine invited me to get a gym membership. We committed to a class that met three days a week. At 6:00 AM. And they encouraged you to get there early. At 5:45 AM. And it was twenty minutes away. When you aren't used to that type of schedule, which I wasn't, it can be very tempting to hit the snooze button and go "next time." But, as you reach for that snooze button, you remember: your friend will be there. He is probably getting ready to head over right now. He's expecting you. So, you get in the car, crank the *Rocky* theme music, and drive over. We stayed in this class for several months, and we rarely missed.

As 1 Tim 4:8 says, "Physical training is of some value, but godliness has value for all things, holding promise for both the present life and the life to come." Health—physical, emotional, and spiritual—requires discipline, and discipline is best cultivated alongside others. We need one another to be strong when we are weak, and to point us to Jesus. Having friends who will ask about your spiritual life (and who won't accept a surface level answer) are pivotal in drawing us to Jesus. God designed us to be encouraged, challenged, corrected, and built up together.

In these conversations, community also provides insights and perspectives different from our own. We need to gather around the word together, actually reading and discussing Scripture beyond a sermon, podcast, or audio book. There is something special about believers interacting with one another through the Bible. Jesus is present when Christians gather, and we believe he speaks in a unique way in that context. If we don't meet with other Christians intentionally, we are missing out on a facet of God's communication. We will talk more about what this practically looks like in a later chapter, but we also want to acknowledge other sources of community that can be easily overlooked.

Global Diversity: The Global Church

Christianity is a global family. There are believers on every continent, and, if we truly believe that we are one part of many in the body of Christ, we need each other. We can't look at another location or culture and say, "I don't need you." The Bible is God's revealed truth to the world, and we gain new perspectives when we look at Scripture through the eyes of others.

Biblical scholar Craig Keener states, "Readers today often have cultural blind spots that can be helpfully addressed by believers in other cultures."[3] In his work, he gives some examples that help make this more concrete:

> Messianic Jewish believers, for example, rightly call gentile Christians' attention to positive texts about the law or the Jewish people that we have historically neglected. Because of traditional Confucian values, Chinese and Korean believers rightly highlight for Westerners the values of honor and respect found in Scripture. On the other hand, some revolutionary contexts in Latin America may invite emphases on justice and liberation that prophetically challenge authority. The Confessing Church in Nazi Germany and antiapartheid Christians in South Africa rightly raised challenges to churches subservient to demonic political ideologies. Too often Christian readings domesticate the Bible in ways acceptable to our own contexts, but listening to Christians from different settings helps challenge our hermeneutical[4] blind spots and canons within the canon.[5]

---

3. Keener, "Pentecostal Biblical Interpretation," 279.
4. "Hermeneutical" meaning how we interpret the Bible.
5. Keener, "Pentecostal Biblical Interpretation," 279.

Part I: Why We Need To Live In The Text

We can easily assume that our tradition is the greatest expression of the Christian faith. More advanced. More refined. More educated. More true. And we may never put this belief to words—it is just an underlying assumption that blinds us to our need for one another. But even beyond our location and tradition, we can assume that our *time* is the greatest version of Christianity.

Chronological Diversity: The Historic Church

Hebrews 12:1 states that we are surrounded by a "great cloud of witnesses." The writer of the book had just finished sharing the stories of biblical heroes like Abraham, Sarah, Moses, and Rahab, but this cloud of witnesses includes all those who have gone before us in Jesus. And, although it may feel strange to some, what if we believed we could learn something from the historic church beyond what not to do? Ancient writers and thinkers have something to offer us, and we have "chronological snobbery" if we believe that the present way of thinking is inherently better.

C. S. Lewis defined chronological snobbery as "the uncritical acceptance of the intellectual climate common to our own age and the assumption that whatever has gone out of date is on that account discredited."[6] Basically, this means that we look at Christians from the Roman era, the middle ages, the Renaissance, and the following generations up until ours, and believe that they offer little to nothing of benefit to us today. Now, it can feel overwhelming when you think about listening to two thousand years of opinions, but our encouragement is to start small. Here are some of our reading suggestions from different periods of the faith:

- Augustine, *Confessions*
- Athanasius, *On the Incarnation*
- Thomas à Kempis, *The Imitation of Christ*
- Bonhoeffer, *The Cost of Discipleship*
- Shelley, *Church History in Plain Language*

6. Lindsley, "C. S. Lewis on Chronological Snobbery."

Relationship: Knowing Each Other

Another important point to keep in mind: this is not just a study group. We don't only need to know Jesus and the Bible more. We need to know each other. It is great to have different perspectives on a passage of Scripture. We all bring something unique to the table because of our experiences, personalities, and knowledge, but a communal mindset means something greater. It means knowing one another's stories. It is sharing your joys and challenges with one another, approaching the Bible as people, not just students.

Living in the text means being invested in one another's lives. The Bible tells us that we are brothers and sisters, and that we are to carry each other's burdens. If we want to grow closer to Jesus, we need to grow closer with other Christians. This isn't always convenient or easy. People aren't always convenient or easy. Investing financially requires money, and investing relationally requires effort and vulnerability. It takes time to build and maintain friendships, and friendships are one of the contexts in which we should interact with the word.

Reaching: Sharing the News

Christianity isn't a closed social group. The heart of this movement and of our lives is the incarnation, death, and resurrection of Jesus Christ. This outward focus needs to be stated. If we truly are to follow Jesus and live in his life, we need to share the good news. Living in the text does not just mean that we are maturing as individuals and have a close-knit community of other Christians we enjoy doing life with. If our mindset halts at that point, we have missed Jesus.

The word of God needs to be communicated to others. Studying and meditating are not like other disciplines such as working out or eating healthy, being self-centered. The end goal of our life in the text is to know Jesus and make him known. You need to know the word for *others*. We are called to sacrificially love and serve broken people just as Jesus did. We believe that he lives in

Part I: Why We Need To Live In The Text

and through us. If that is the case, we need to act like what we are: the hands and feet of Jesus. The Bible is communal because it is not meant to be only studied and memorized in private. The word should lead us to actually tell the story of Jesus to those who don't know him.

THE COMMUNITY'S SPIRITUAL FOUNDATION

God designed his word to be the rallying point for his people. It is what we gather around as we serve and love Jesus. The books of Ezra and Nehemiah tell the story of God's people, the Israelites, returning to Jerusalem from exile. The entire second chapter of Ezra is devoted to recounting the logistics of the journey:

> The list of the men of the people of Israel:
> the descendants of Parosh 2,172
> of Shephatiah 372
> of Arah 775
> of Pahath-Moab (through the line of Jeshua and Joab) 2,812.

And it goes on for a while. The author describes the number of people from the different tribes and the number of priests, musicians, door keepers, and servants. The book is titled "Ezra," but it is about much more than one man. This is the community returning to the capital of the promised land.

When they arrived, the group began to rebuild the temple throughout the reign of several different rulers. It took years because of opposition from other groups and leaders, but it was finally completed. After all this happened, Ezra, who was a teacher of the law, came to Jerusalem from Babylon with another group of exiles returning home. Ezra then set about teaching God's instructions to the people.

In Neh 7 and 8, all the people were brought together in Jerusalem to hear the Law of the Lord read. This would have included the Torah, the first five books of the Bible. As Ezra read the Law, other Levites (those of the priestly tribe) taught the people, "making it clear and giving the meaning so that the people understood what was being read" (Neh 8:8). This chapter tells us that the crowd consisted of "men, women, and others who could understand" (Neh 8:3). Imagine the scene: one guy up on a platform reading the stories of Genesis, Exodus, Leviticus, Deuteronomy, and Numbers to men, women, and children. Then, a group of other men walks through the crowd explaining what is being read. And this continues for hours, from dawn to noon. When they finished, they dispersed to celebrate the teaching with good food and drink. It was a happy day.

The community was foundational to every stage of rebuilding Jerusalem, from the exiles returning in groups to rebuilding the temple together to the corporate instruction of God's word. At no point was this process or message about one person alone. The context was always community, and that context has gone on to influence Christians since the days Jesus walked and lived with his disciples.

LIFE TOGETHER

Have you ever heard of the illegal seminaries of Nazi Germany? As the lines blurred between the German church and the Nazi party, Christians began to form secret seminaries where the next generation of ministers could be trained. Dietrich Bonhoeffer spearheaded the effort and oversaw several groups of students in their studies. However, these seminaries were much more than classrooms; they became a lifestyle. Bonhoeffer lived with the students, chose to be called "Brother" rather than "Director," and guided them through a rhythm in the word and in community. The group would rise in silence so that the first words spoken in the day were from Scripture. They shared meals and work together. They were assigned a partner to confide in and confess their struggles.[7] For Bonhoeffer and his students, following Jesus was about far more than gaining information. Although these schools were ultimately shut down by the government, the lessons learned remained with

---

7. Metaxas, *Bonhoeffer*, 262–73.

the students. Living in the text was a relational lifestyle of knowing one another and God in the context of Scripture. The two were connected.

How often do we interact with the Bible in community? Do we truly believe we need one another to follow our Savior and to live in his word? We can't do this alone. We aren't supposed to. The scrolls of the Bible are designed to be read, processed, discussed, and understood within the connected body of Christ. We cannot afford to ignore the wisdom and strength the Holy Spirit has for us in one another. The Bible belongs to the community.

SUMMARY POINTS

- The context of a work shapes its meaning. Authorship, intended audience, location, time, and surrounding details all impact one's understanding, or lack thereof, of the work.
- We often read the Bible like it was written *to* us. It's not, though it is written *for* us. There is a difference between the two that vastly changes how we should read it.
- Only three of the sixty-six books in the Bible were written to individuals, and even those have been shared and read to the body of Christ at large. The rest of the books are poetry, history, or letters intended for groups of people.
- In the Western church, we often read the Bible through an individualistic lens. We ask, "What does this mean for me?" rather than the church at large. We also think that the most important time in the word is our own personal time alone, rather than in the community.
- Studying and praying in private are great disciplines that we should commit ourselves to, but we should not isolate ourselves from brothers and sisters.

The Bible Is Communal

- Approaching the Bible in community is helpful for:

    a. *Learning: Studying the Word*
    Biblical community provides accountability, interaction, encouragement, protection, and healthy discomfort. The group provides insights and perspectives that we will miss by ourselves. We learn better together.

    b. *Global Diversity: The Global Church*
    There are Christians on every continent with different cultures, strengths, and blind spots. We get a fuller picture of God and the Bible when we consider perspectives different than ours.

    c. *Chronological Diversity: The Historic Church*
    Christians from other times also give us insights into the word. An opinion isn't less valuable because it is old. Although there may be weaknesses or things we disagree with, there will also be truth and treasures in the historic church. People have walked with Jesus for two thousand years. We can learn from them.

    d. *Relationship: Knowing Each Other*
    Living in the word together is more than a study group. We are first and foremost brothers and sisters. Living in community means knowing one another and being known, encouraging and bearing one another's burdens. We do life together.

    e. *Reaching: Sharing the News*
    We know the word to make Jesus known to others. The central message of Jesus is God reaching to restore his creation. Our studies, growth, and maturity should lead to sharing the good news of Jesus with those who do not know him.

- God's work through the Israelites in Ezra and Nehemiah was completely communal. The people returned to the promised land, rebuilt the temple, and learned from the word together.

Part I: Why We Need To Live In The Text

- Dietrich Bonhoeffer and the illegal seminaries in Germany embodied this communal mindset. Rather than simple classrooms, the seminaries were marked by relationships, vulnerability, and attention to the word and prayer.
- We can't do this alone. We need to walk with other believers in the word, remaining in Christ together by being a part of his body. The Bible belongs to the community.

PART II
Living Out the Text

> Then the king called together all the elders of Judah and Jerusalem. He went up to the temple of the LORD with the people of Judah, the inhabitants of Jerusalem, the priests and the Levites—all the people from the least to the greatest. He read in their hearing all the words of the Book of the Covenant, which had been found in the temple of the LORD. The king stood by his pillar and renewed the covenant in the presence of the LORD—to follow the LORD and keep his commands, statutes and decrees with all his heart and all his soul, and to obey the words of the covenant written in this book. Then he had everyone in Jerusalem and Benjamin pledge themselves to it; the people of Jerusalem did this in accordance with the covenant of God, the God of their ancestors.
> —2 CHRONICLES 34:29–32

The approach to Scripture that we are suggesting is not a new idea. It is rooted in the revelations and examples we see in the nation of Israel in the Old Testament, the life of Jesus and the formation of the church in the New Testament, and the example of Christians throughout history. However, living in the text is not just a historical study. The Spirit who speaks through the word is still transforming lives, including ours. That's why we're writing this book.

All of history is his story—HIStory. The foundation of our individual stories is the overarching tale of the Bible and all creation: "In the beginning, God . . ." (Gen 1:1). The Bible is about him. We need to understand that to accurately live in the text. He is the main character, not us. This is his story, but did you know that Jesus invites you to take part in the story? "True Christianity is the life that Jesus lived in the past, lived out in you in the present."[1] When we realize and accept this, we are free to be all he made us to be: renewed people united with him.

Living in the text reflects Jesus himself as it is both human and divine: the merging of our story with God's. We need to know his to truly know ours. In this section, we include the overarching story of the Bible that points to Jesus, followed by our own stories of how God saved and remade us through the word. Our stories point to him as the Author and Finisher, First and Last, Alpha and Omega. Our prayer is that you are encouraged to recognize God's story in your own life as you read about ours.

The Bible is needed. It is ignored in society. It is a communal book. However, living in Jesus is much more than following a teaching, establishing healthy habits, or doing "better." It is walking in a daily, loving relationship in and with the God who made you and remade you in Christ. It is living out his story in your own.

---

1. Sweet and Viola, *Jesus Manifesto*, 59.

4

HIStory Revealed

> And yet just because it is a book about both the sublime and the unspeakable, it is a book also about life, the way it really is. It is a book about people who at one and the same time can be both believing and unbelieving, innocent and guilty, crusaders and crooks, full of hope and full of despair. In other words, it is a book about us. And it is a book about God. If it is not about the God we believe in, then it is about the God we do not believe in. One way or another, the story we find in the Bible is our own story. —Frederick Buechner[1]

THE BIBLE: HISTORY

The word of God is exactly that: his word. And because of this fact, it is his story. HIStory. The story of all of history is about him, told by him through the voices of others via miraculous and mysterious inspiration, preserved through sacred writing—The Bible. The tale takes place over thousands of years, with many characters—some like us, some different—every one of them sucked into the vortex that is him. In Deut 6:4–8 (NRSV), God would emphatically command his people, Israel, the ones who had been

---

1. Buechner, *Wishful Thinking*, 9.

Part II: Living Out The Text

sucked into the center of his story, to remember the ancient and timeless journey in which they found themselves:

> Hear, O Israel: The LORD is our God, the LORD alone. You shall love the LORD your God with all your heart and with all your soul and with all your might. Keep these words that I am commanding you today in your heart. Recite them to your children and talk about them when you are at home and when you are away, when you lie down and when you rise. Bind them as a sign on your hand, fix them as an emblem on your forehead, and write them on the doorposts of your house and on your gates.

Keep. Recite. Talk. Bind. Fix. His people were to show total commitment and love for God and his word in a myriad of ways. They were to perpetuate HIStory daily, wholeheartedly, and holistically—telling it in their homes and then writing it on the physical structures. They were to attach portions of it to their bodies—taking it with them to work and the marketplace. They were to tell it to their children in the morning when the sun (that he had created) rose with the dawn, then at bedtime when it set again: remember, remember, remember. Archaeologist Dr. Randall Price sheds light on the nature and purpose of this wholehearted commitment:

> "We are what we remember," and "What we remember affects who we are and what we experience in life." This is especially true of our spiritual lives because what we remember about God forms the foundation for our faith. In the Torah (Genesis through Deuteronomy), God repeatedly commands his people to "remember" in order to obey Him (Ex. 13:3; 20:8; Dt. 5:15; 8:2, 18; 9:7; 16:12; 32:7). Deuteronomy 6:4–5 gave Israel a brief statement of faith, one Jesus called "the first [foremost] of all the commandments" (Mk. 12:29) and one known to every Jewish person as the Shema. Deuteronomy 6:7–9 tells the Israelites to remember by making the Scriptures the focus of their lives, instructing them, "You shall write them on the doorposts [Hebrew, mezuzot; plural of mezuzah] of your house and on your gates" (v. 9).[2]

---

2. Price, "Reminder to Remember" (brackets original).

The mezuzah commandment, as it came to be known, was a mandate for spiritual application (Prov 6:21) and became a literal family observance in the Jewish culture. The observance first appears in Scripture regarding the doorpost where the blood of the Passover lamb was applied (Exod 12:7, 22, 23). A physical demonstration of obedience, visible at the entrance to the home, was what set the people inside apart as belonging to the Lord. These are some of the most foundational words of the story—God's story. It is the one in which all of us find ourselves and it is the one that the Author, God himself, wants to affect every aspect of our lives—where we live, where we work, and the people with whom we live and work. It may not be that we're supposed to wear boxes on our foreheads anymore, but we are to stand out on his behalf. That begs of us the questions: How might we be standing out in our communities, homes, or places of work? And, for what do we stand—or more importantly—for whom?

HISTORY CONNECTED

Have you ever had your mind blown by a book, movie, or TV show? You know the ones that, when you get to the end, make you understand the rest of the story in a whole new light. It's the moment everything clicks and makes you want to read or watch the story again because it all makes so much sense now. Some popular movies capture this feeling, like *The Prestige*, *Interstellar*, and *Tenet* (all of these happen to be directed by Christopher Nolan, who seems to like this type of storytelling). In good storytelling, the end of a tale not only completes the beginning, but brings new meaning to the entire work.

However, it seems many don't see the Bible in this manner. Maybe it's because they already know how the story goes (or think they do). Too often it's viewed only as a tragic story of sacrifice that ended on a hill outside of Jerusalem, with a resurrection of some sort three days later. While these things are partly true, HIStory is so much more. It's an intricate, epic tale that is both tragic and victorious, a story focused upon the single most important life ever to have been lived on planet earth—the life, death, resurrection, and establishment of the kingdom of Jesus Christ. Every teaching, every healing, every action, and every detail of his life were specifically ordered and completed through the fulfillment of hundreds of Old Testament prophecies. According to God's plan from the beginning of time, in spite of Satan's repeated efforts against it, Jesus was victorious. The Old Testament pointed towards Jesus' coming, and the New Testament proclaims that he has done so and will ultimately come again to rule as King for all of eternity.

The story of Jesus is not only played out in the New Testament—it is much more ancient than that. It is one that involves the first inhabitants of the planet, Adam and Eve, engaging in conversation in God's garden with a serpent who could communicate. This communication would result in sin, sickness, and death entering the story—and that's only three chapters into the epic tale (see Gen 3). However, God himself would take matters into his own hands in Gen 3:14–15 and make a proclamation as to how this cataclysmic wrong would ultimately be made right. It is quite literally the thesis and road map for the rest of the story. If you don't already know what a thesis is, it's "the main idea, opinion, or theory of a person, group, piece of writing, or speech."[3] So, here is God's thesis for HIStory, uttered by his own voice, while Adam and Eve hid in shame. The deceitful serpent stood speechless next to them, just before he was cursed to "crawl on his belly":

> So the LORD God said to the serpent, "Because you have done this, Cursed are you above all livestock and all wild animals! You will crawl on your belly and you will eat dust all the days of your life. And I will put enmity between you and the woman, and between your offspring [seed] and hers; he will crush your head, and you will strike his heel." (Gen 3:14–15)

Many readers of the story miss the magnitude of the proclamations contained in these few verses. Through them, the stage is set for the rest of the books and characters contained in the entire

---

3. *Cambridge Dictionary*, "Thesis."

Bible, as well as for those who would come after, including you and me. Those who would have faith in God's word here and throughout all of history would be included in this serpent-crushing prophecy. The "he" in verse 15 would be none other than Jesus, the one to whom the apostle Paul would eventually refer in 1 Cor 15:45 (NRSV) as a "last [second] Adam":

> Thus it is written, "The first man, Adam, became a living being"; the last Adam became a life-giving spirit.

The second Adam would succeed where the first one failed. The first passed his fallen, sinful, dying nature to all of his seed—every person born thereafter, up to this very moment in time. Jesus, God's seed, would eventually be born through Mary to give new, fresh, and eternal hope to all throughout the ages who would, by faith, follow him. That's why it is important to pay attention to the lineage of Jesus in both Matt 1:1–17 and Luke 3:21–38. These are the records of the seed being passed forward through the ages, through the men and women who were used by God as a result of their faith. As one reads the story, they will see that God didn't use perfect lives. Rather he used people because of his grace, including those who put their faith in him.

While the stories of all who would follow him in faith aren't included in the Bible, we'll now take a look at a few of the most prominent. God established three covenants, or agreements, with different men that defined God's relationship with humanity.

COVENANT #1: ABRAHAM "ALL PEOPLE ON EARTH WILL BE BLESSED THROUGH YOU"

First is a man who entered into a faith covenant with God: Abram.

> The LORD had said to Abram, "Go from your country, your people and your father's household to the land I will show you. I will make you into a great nation, and I will bless you; I will make your name great, and you will be a blessing. I will bless those who bless you, and whoever curses you I will curse; and all peoples on earth will be

PART II: LIVING OUT THE TEXT

> blessed through you." . . . So Abram went, as the LORD had told him; and Lot went with him. Abram was seventy-five years old when he set out from Harran. . . . The LORD appeared to Abram and said, "To your offspring I will give this land." So he built an altar there to the LORD, who had appeared to him. . . . Then Abram set out. (Gen 12:4, 7, 9)

God has kept his promise to make Abram into a great nation and to bless him immeasurably. He changed Abram's name to Abraham, stating that the world would be blessed through his descendants. This commitment stands as a pillar of God's nature as a covenant keeper. Abraham's descendants became God's people, and through Abraham's faith, the serpent crushing seed that would bless all people on earth passed through time.

COVENANT #2: MOSES "A KINGDOM OF PRIESTS AND A HOLY NATION"

Abraham's family grew and spread over generations. However, they were eventually enslaved in Egypt. God used a man named Moses to deliver the Hebrews from bondage. After bringing them out, God called Moses up a mountain to give them the Law and establish another covenant with his people:

> Then Moses went up to God, and the LORD called to him from the mountain and said, "This is what you are to say to the descendants of Jacob and what you are to tell the people of Israel: 'You yourselves have seen what I did to Egypt, and how I carried you on eagles' wings and brought you to myself. Now if you obey me fully and keep my covenant, then out of all nations you will be my treasured possession. Although the whole earth is mine, you will be for me a kingdom of priests and a holy nation.' These are the words you are to speak to the Israelites." So Moses went back and summoned the elders of the people and set before them all the words the LORD had commanded him to speak. The people all responded together, "We will do everything the LORD has said." So

> Moses brought their answer back to the LORD. The LORD said to Moses, "I am going to come to you in a dense cloud, so that the people will hear me speaking with you and will always put their trust in you." Then Moses told the LORD what the people had said. (Exod 19:3–9)

In spite of the inability of Israel to hold up their end of the bargain, and Moses' recurrent frustration with them, he and they were used to pass the seed forward. They were God's treasured possession. They would be the people from which the serpent crushing seed would come—a seed that would result not merely in an earthly hope, but an eternal one. That seed would fulfill and establish a renewed kingdom of priests and holy nation.

COVENANT #3: DAVID "THE SON OF DAVID'S ETERNAL THRONE"

After the Israelites settled in the promised land, God established David as king over the nation. He was known as a man after God's own heart, and he would, by faith, follow God through some trying, some victorious, and some glorious times. Even the secular world knows the story of his triumph over the giant Goliath. God especially loved David, so much so that the second Adam would be called on numerous occasions, "Son of David." The Lord made this covenant with the shepherd king:

> When your days are over and you go to be with your ancestors, I will raise up your offspring to succeed you, one of your own sons, and I will establish his kingdom. He is the one who will build a house for me, and I will establish his throne forever. I will be his father, and he will be my son. I will never take my love away from him, as I took it away from your predecessor. I will set him over my house and my kingdom forever; his throne will be established forever. (1 Chr 17:11–14)

This covenant would be confirmed again, by David's son, Solomon:

> Now, LORD, the God of Israel, keep for your servant David my father the promises you made to him when you said, "You shall never fail to have a successor to sit before me on the throne of Israel, if only your descendants are careful in all they do to walk before me according to my law, as you have done." (2 Chr 6:16)

God would ultimately express his love, power, and authority over the world through an eternal king, one who was of David's line.

COVENANTS FULFILLED

Because the men called by God into the above covenant relationships were of Adam's seed, they were unable to perfectly keep their sides of the agreements with God—so he would have to do that as well. Yes, he would need to keep both sides of any and all covenants made with anyone who was the seed of Adam. Thus, Jesus came into the world as God-become-man. In Gal 4:4–7, the apostle Paul affirmed that Jesus was the one and only being who could do such a thing. When the time was ready, he was born of a woman, Mary, and fulfilled all God had promised. Jesus is the fulfillment of God's covenant with Abraham to bless the world, God's covenant with Moses to establish a royal priesthood and holy nation, and God's covenant with David to raise up an eternal king from his line. It all culminates in Jesus.

However, Christ did not only fulfill the covenants of the Old Testament. He also establishes a new agreement between God and humanity. The writer of Hebrews would point towards this in Heb 9:15 and 24[4]:

> For this reason Christ is the mediator of a new covenant, that those who are called may receive the promised eternal inheritance—now that he has died as a ransom to set them free from the sins committed under the first covenant. . . . For Christ did not enter a sanctuary made with human hands that was only a copy of the true one;

---

4. Also in 4:14–16, 5:7–10, and 6:13–20.

he entered heaven itself, now to appear for us in God's presence.

The apostle John describes this mediator, Jesus of Nazareth, in the first eighteen verses of his Gospel. This passage is known as the prologue, and in it John states that Jesus is:

- *The Word*: Jesus is God's message, power, and identity become flesh. He was with God in the beginning and is God. All things were made through him.
- *The Light*: Jesus is the one who brings light and life to all who receive him, giving them the right to become children of God.
- *The Source of Grace and Truth*: Jesus is the unveiling of God's ultimate forgiveness and identity, fulfilling the Law of Moses and revealing the Father to humanity.

The title of this chapter is "HIStory Revealed." There are two parts (or persons) to how the New Testament reveals the foundational message of all history. The first is Jesus. If we are to live in the text, we need to always keep him at the center of our hearts and minds. Studying the Bible isn't just an exercise to learn an ancient book. Because, in the most respectful way possible, the Bible is a means to an end. That end is to know Jesus.

After Jesus resurrected, he appeared to two disciples as they walked from Jerusalem to a town called Emmaus. Not knowing it was Jesus, they proceeded to tell him all about his own ministry, trial, and execution. They were confused because they thought Jesus would fulfill the Old Testament covenants by establishing an earthly kingdom in the nation of Israel, but instead he was killed. For some reason, others said that Jesus' tomb was empty. What were they to think?

> He said to them, "How foolish you are, and how slow to believe all that the prophets have spoken! Did not the Messiah have to suffer these things and then enter his glory?" And beginning with Moses and all the Prophets, he explained to them what was said in all the Scriptures concerning himself. (Luke 24:25–27)

Part II: Living Out The Text

We know that Emmaus is around seven miles from Jerusalem. We don't know where they were in their journey, but Jesus walked them through a lot. Everything that they had known since they were children was suddenly explained as pointing to him. Creation, humanity's sin, God's promises, the formation of their people group, every belief and hope their ancestors had clung to through centuries now standing in front of them. It's that end-of-the-story-plot-twist feeling. Imagine what it must have been like to have God himself look you in the eye and say, "This is what that means: I AM that I AM!"

It all points to Jesus. All of it. This may sound repetitive, and that is intentional. If you attend a church, listen to worship music, read spiritual books, or practice spiritual disciplines regularly, how often is Jesus at the center? For example, you could hear a sermon series on relationships, finances, politics, volunteering, or spiritual gifts. You could sing a song that, for some reason, talks more about yourself than God. You could pick up a book by your favorite leader and end up more impressed with them, focused on your own benefit, or simply entertained. You could give to your church, serve the homeless, read your Bible, and attend a small group all without even thinking of Jesus. How often do we miss Christ in these things?

The Bible does offer wisdom for every area of life, but none of these things should be pursued without Jesus. He is history and truth revealed. In our faith, any sermon, song, book, or action that is engaged with apart from a foundation firmly on Christ is misplaced. Christianity is not about being good people, living our best life, or being physically, emotionally, and socially healthy. It is about Jesus, but we cannot force our hearts and minds to surrender to Christ in our own strength. This is why we need the next person of the Trinity for the word to be revealed to us: the Holy Spirit.

WE NEED THE ADVOCATE

A few weeks after Jesus resurrected, he instructed his followers to wait before beginning their mission to share this good news with the world. They needed something, or someone, in order to accomplish all God had given them. Jesus had already referenced this before his death:

> But the Advocate, the Holy Spirit, whom the Father will send in my name, will teach you all things and will remind you of everything I have said to you. (John 14:26)

God's story isn't simply the payment for our sin; it's him giving us his life. And it is scandalous, far more than we often think. Imagine someone who made a living from killing innocent people. They would go from place to place, murdering innocent men, women, and children. These are horrendous crimes that are difficult to process from the outside, much less from firsthand experience. Think of terrorists, kidnappers, and traffickers. What would you expect if they were brought to trial by those they had harmed? How would you feel if the judge let them go free without a single consequence? Even more, what if they were given more money than you could ever dream of and a place of authority to live in luxury for the rest of their lives?

We are much more like these "bad" people than we are God. In sin, our guilt places us unfathomably below God's standard of holiness and righteousness. And the gift he gives us is even more amazing than the example above. We could never deserve forgiveness, but God shows us his mercy. Then, the brokenness and shame we once had is replaced by his perfect, divine, unfathomably wonderful life. Are you getting the picture? Do you get a glimpse of the amazing gift God offers in his presence?

God chose to give us his Spirit through Jesus. We cannot live in him without the Spirit. The Spirit is the one who teaches us about Jesus and makes us more like him. First Corinthians 2:11–16 states:

Part II: Living Out The Text

> For who knows a person's thoughts except their own spirit within them? In the same way no one knows the thoughts of God except the Spirit of God. What we have received is not the spirit of the world, but the Spirit who is from God, so that we may understand what God has freely given us. This is what we speak, not in words taught us by human wisdom but in words taught by the Spirit, explaining spiritual realities with Spirit-taught words. The person without the Spirit does not accept the things that come from the Spirit of God but considers them foolishness, and cannot understand them because they are discerned only through the Spirit. The person with the Spirit makes judgments about all things, but such a person is not subject to merely human judgments, for, "Who has known the mind of the Lord so as to instruct him?" But we have the mind of Christ.

The Bible points to Jesus, but we can only comprehend that through the empowerment of the Holy Spirit. Anyone can study Scripture and learn things from the text, but only those who have God's Spirit will understand it in a life-transformative and divine way. Through him, we are brought to life, regenerated by the same Spirit that raised Jesus from the dead.

Living in the text is truly living in Jesus through the Spirit. We breathe in Jesus, he breathes through us. We walk in Jesus, he walks through us. We live in Jesus, he lives through us. That is the point of all of history. The apostle Paul put it this way:

> I have been crucified with Christ and I no longer live, but Christ lives in me. The life I now live in the body, I live by faith in the Son of God, who loved me and gave himself for me. (Gal 2:20)

This is HIStory. But, because the story is about Jesus, it is about us. Leonard Sweet and Frank Viola describe this as a "coauthored narrative process."[5] We live out our lives in a loving partnership with Christ. Scripture's story continues through us, God's people, as we remain in Jesus.

---

5. Sweet and Viola, *Jesus Manifesto*, 68–69.

SUMMARY POINTS

- The Bible and all of history show that we are living in God's story. It is HIStory. This is all about him. He is the main character. We are not.

- God repeatedly commanded his people to "remember" his word. They were to discuss it, share it with their children, and meditate on it regularly.

- This story culminates in the life, death, resurrection, and establishment of the kingdom of Jesus Christ. However, the story began in the garden of Eden when Adam and Eve sinned. God proclaimed the serpent who had tempted them would ultimately be crushed by the seed of the woman. God would fulfill this statement through the people of Israel.

- God defined his relationship with and salvation through Israel in three important covenants, or agreements:

    1. *Abraham:* God chose Abraham and his family to be his people. God promised to bless the world through Abraham's descendants.
    2. *Moses:* God gave Israel the Law and proclaimed they would be his royal priests and a holy nation.
    3. *David:* God promised David that one of his descendants would rule over the world on God's behalf for eternity.

- Jesus fulfilled each of these as the means by which the world is blessed, by being the faithful Israelite who represented God to the world and opened the way for everyone to join his people, and by being the Son of David who will rule forever.

- Jesus also established a new covenant: by faith, anyone who accepts Christ is forgiven of sins and given God's eternal life.

- The first eighteen verses of John are called the prologue. In it, John identifies Jesus as the *Word*, the *Light*, and the *Source of Grace and Truth*.

Part II: Living Out The Text

- The purpose of the Bible is to know Jesus. In Luke 24, Jesus explained to two disciples how the Law and Prophets of the Old Testament point to him.
- We should be Christocentric (Christ-centered) in all that we do. Our studies, sermons, work, prayer, rest, and everything else should be founded upon Jesus.
- In order to understand the word and live in the life of Christ, we need the Holy Spirit. Jesus commanded his disciples to wait in Jerusalem for the gift from the Father. They weren't to begin sharing the good news until they were filled with God's divine presence.
- God giving us his life is a scandalous and awe-inspiring gift. We do not deserve his forgiveness nor his love, but he chooses to give his people his very presence. We cannot live in Jesus without the Spirit.
- God invites us to live in his life, not just follow his rules. Living in the text is a dynamic relationship with God through Jesus.

5

Jeff's Story

> Meet God face to face.
> —Baptist Brigade Boys Summer Backpacking Trip Flier, 1974

THE ABOVE QUOTE WAS printed on a flier that I vividly remember seeing as a twelve-year-old wilderness greenhorn, who had just recently given his heart to Jesus. The God thing wasn't the most alluring aspect of the flier though—it was the Rocky Mountains. While the Christian faith was still new to me and my family, the mountains weren't. We had traveled west to vacation in them on a yearly basis, even when we didn't live in Colorado. Now that we had moved to the foothills of the Rockies, they were an ever-present reality that called to me daily as I looked to the west each morning. The prospect of meeting God in the Rockies was my kind of outing and a life-altering one it would be.

While backpacking in the mountains would certainly be a new experience for me, self-assurance wasn't. For some reason, I was born with a fair amount of confidence, and my parents did a great job at fostering it—maybe to a fault. While my twelve-year-old confident young self thought that I was ready to totally engage with the mountains—walking, sleeping, hiking, and eating in them—I really wasn't even close to being ready. Our leader was an accomplished and experienced mountaineer, and he had

Part II: Living Out The Text

repeatedly given us written and verbal instructions about wilderness survival in our weekly Baptist Brigade Boys troop meetings. I remember thinking to myself, "How hard could running around and having a blast in the mountains really be?" As I would soon find out, it could be very, very hard—sometimes dangerously so.

After bidding our parents goodbye in the parking lot of First Baptist Church, we headed west towards the Gore Wilderness Area. The energy created by myself and the ten other twelve-year-olds in that old church van made the two hour trip seem like ten minutes. Bounding out of the vehicle upon arrival at the trailhead, we peered up at a group of jagged peaks known as the Eagle's Nest—perched in all their glory at over eleven thousand feet. A snowcapped landmass called Elliot's Ridge fanned from the Nest to the north, a glacial ice bridge that was interspersed with patches of verdant high country pasture.

Our leader pointed up at the ominous rocks and explained that we would be heading that way early the next morning. He also repeated some of the rules that I previously ignored, as the mountains and my confidence were clouding my ability to hear. Had I listened more intently, I would have heard that I was never, ever to go off on my own—especially without my whistle. A whistle was mandatory equipment, as it could be blown in case of emergency. I was also supposed to always have my water bottle with me, in addition to a map and compass—which I hadn't learned to use very proficiently. After being placed in groups of three buddies, we were told to "ALWAYS, ALWAYS, ALWAYS" stay with and/or inform those buddies of our whereabouts. The final encouragement was that if these rules were obeyed, we would be safe, have fun, meet God face to face, and live to tell about it.

Sleeping was hard that first night—literally very hard as I tried to doze off while lying in my sleeping bag on top of a one-inch-thick foam liner that had been hastily placed on the floor of our tent, which had been hastily pitched on a stump and a couple of rocks. After telling spooky mountain stories and dumb jokes that were middle-school-hilarious, we dozed off sporadically, only to be repeatedly awakened by a cacophony of mysterious night

Jeff's Story

sounds. These unknown sounds were intermittently mixed with bursts of wind and the gurgling waters of Cataract Creek below.

Ultimately, chirping birds welcomed the morning as the Sun followed closely behind, announcing a new day by peeking through the morning haze that rested like a comfy blanket over Eagle's Nest. We followed suit by peeking out of our bags into the frigid mountain morning. Breakfast was frigid, too. We were told not to light a fire, due to the fact that we had a lot of ground to cover on our first day. Our hurried breakfast consisted of a packet of instant Quaker Oats, brought to life with half a cup of boiling water, and a frozen protein bar that tasted like plastic, with everything being washed down by an extremely tart orange juice substitute called Tang. Breaking camp was certainly a new challenge. It was the first time I realized gear just didn't fit back into a pack the same as it did several days before. Excitement, cold middle-school-sized hands, and Elliot's Ridge beckoning over your shoulder to "hurry up" certainly muddled the re-packing process.

Finally, it was time to hit the trail and, due to my previously mentioned confidence level, I had worn down our leader and convinced him that I should be the first in line. After giving me some important instructions that I listened to vaguely, our group of three was off like a shot from a starter's pistol. Laughing, throwing rocks, and kicking sticks, our little posse came to fork in the trail after fork in the trail, obediently turning right as I thought that I heard our leader instruct. However, had I listened more intently to the exact instructions he had given me, I would have remembered that we were to take every right turn where the tree had been marked by an "ax cut." An ax cut is a mark made about six feet off the ground to indicate which way to turn at a fork in the trail. Blazing past ax-marked tree after ax-marked tree, we had actually been following what is known as a "game trail." Game trails are not main trails that lead to particular, known, human-established destinations, but trails used by animals in the wilderness for finding food and water. One can only imagine what our little team thought when we came to a trail that ended at an outcropping of rocks that gave no opportunity to turn right. What were we to do?

Part II: Living Out The Text

Increased heart rate from being at high altitude decreases the amount of oxygen to the brain, which also decreases one's ability to make good decisions—and that was exactly what happened to us that day. Adding fear to the equation made things exponentially worse. In this physical and emotional state, we three twelve-year-olds began to make about every mistake that could be made when one is lost. Had we listened to our leader, we would have known that when you're lost, it is always best to sit down immediately, clear your head, blow your whistle, then take out your map and compass to get a grasp on your bearings. However, none of us were proficient in navigation, we forgot to blow our whistles, and it was getting late in the day—fear, hunger, and fatigue were setting in. After backtracking several times, we found ourselves even more fatigued, more afraid, and more lost. Fortunately, we made one good decision that day, which was to stop when it got so dark that we couldn't really see the trail anymore. Hastily, we set up our tent on the side of a mountain, crawled into our sleeping bags, and tried to sleep—lost and afraid on a mountainside below Elliot's Ridge.

That night was both scary and slippery. It was scary because we were desperately lost deep in the wilderness, and slippery because we had set up our tent in the dark, at an extreme angle. The angle caused us to slide to the bottom of the tent every few minutes. When we rolled out the next morning, we weren't really that rested, but at least we were dry and warm from literally sleeping on top of one another. The little sleep we had gotten was punctuated with intermittent dreams of home, Mom's cooking, and warm, soft, flat beds. Once again, breakfast was a rock-hard protein bar and some water.

In an attempt to get the stiffness out of my body and clear my head, I decided to take a short walk. On my walk, I happened to notice that a few yards from where our tent was sitting, there was actually a trail. Walking on it for a few yards, thoughts of home began to rush through my mind. Then, fear hit me like a tsunami. I had not felt fear like this before. It was palpable. I felt as if I was going to die unless I got home at that very moment. Compounding my already dire situation, I made yet another mistake: I decided to extend my morning walk by heading directly for Elliot's Ridge, as it seemed to be right in front of me.

I have learned since that day that things that are big, especially mountains, look much closer than they actually are. I told neither of my buddies what I was doing. I had to get home right that instant. I now know that I was entering a level of extreme panic-induced paranoia that propels many who are lost in the wilderness to their ultimate demise. With no whistle, no map, no compass, no food, and no water (as they were back in my pack), I started to do what is called "wabashing": going cross-country, off trail, over rocks, dead trees, and anything else that's in your way.

Heart pounding rapidly, legs burning furiously, I had to make that ridge that looked oh so close, but was still very far away. In the midst of my panicked state, the terrain actually kind of looked familiar yet different all at the same time. That's what being lost in the wilderness is like: trees and rocks, rocks and trees. The wilderness can be beautiful and inviting, then terrifying and confusing at the same moment. In my lostness, a new sensation came to me—a feeling that I was being watched by something . . . or someone. I was absolutely sure that I was being watched. Was it a mountain lion licking his lips as he stealthily stalked his unsuspecting young prey? Or maybe a bear was waiting for the right moment to have a mid-morning snack. Afraid, head spinning from fear, altitude, hunger, and thirst, I got so tired and defeated that I just plopped down. Thirsty and without a water bottle, I scooped some snow from the drift I happened to have plopped down on and sucked on it. The cool sensation was nice. Morbidly, I began to ponder that if I was being watched by a predator, perhaps it might come and put me out of my misery. Death seemed imminent, certain, and almost welcome.

What would my parents think? My sister? The guys on my little league football team? My youth pastor? What were they all doing down at home as I sat up there on a snow drift waiting to die? What would my funeral be like—and who would come? I really thought that I was going to live longer than this. My stomach growled so loudly that it pulled me out of my momentary visions of an untimely death. Feeling something in the pocket of my flannel shirt, I reached for it. A granola bar perhaps? I was so hungry. Pulling the contents out of my pocket, I found that it wasn't a coveted food source, but a little brown pocket New Testament that my dad had given me a couple of months before. In Dad's newfound faith, he gave anyone and everyone he knew a Bible. The word became his source, and he wanted me to have it as mine. Hungry enough to take a bite out of it, I resisted the temptation and began flipping through some of the pages. It seemed appropriate as I prepared to die up there in the rocks and trees below Elliot's Ridge. On the first page was my dad's signature in his distinctive handwriting: "Presented to: Jeff Voth, on January 31st, 1974." Tears welled up in my eyes as I thought about the fact that my dad had held this same book. What would my parents think when they found my dead body—clutching this little Bible?

I continued flipping, and there on the next page were special scriptures, some of them highlighted in yellow by Dad. There was John 3:16, reminding me that if I believed in Jesus I wouldn't perish, but have everlasting life. I whispered it quietly. I had believed in him only a few months before. Running my finger over Rom 6:23, I whispered words that affirmed that the gift of God was eternal life through Christ Jesus. A little bolt of faith seemed to well up in me as I whispered that one, a little louder this time. I was certain that it applied to me and, since I was getting ready to die, it was somehow comforting. The next verse was Rom 10:13 and it seemed to scream right off the page that whoever called on the name of the Lord would be saved. I had been saved eternally and spiritually earlier in the year, but right there at eleven thousand feet, in the midst of my youthful ignorance, another bolt of faith ignited in me—so much so that I began to not just whisper, but yell the words of the verses into the very thin air up there. I was yelling out to the God I had only recently met. I wondered if these verses might be true physically as well—in that very moment. The echo of my own voice yelling the verses back to me was very heartening.

After yelling the words of the word up to the one who had inspired them, I waited—listened—watched—and wondered. More

Jeff's Story

flickers of hope began rising in my chest; then something beautiful and mysteriously funny happened. The largest mule deer buck I had ever seen calmly sauntered out of the trees and gazed directly at me. Perhaps he was intrigued by the noise, maybe I was sitting on his game trail, or perhaps his Creator had spurred him to let me know that I was not alone. His presence somehow made me feel safe—I wasn't all by myself. Then, something even more mysterious and not funny, but eternally beautiful and impactful occurred. A voice, not from the buck (although that would have been a great addition to the story), permeated the atmosphere—a voice inside of me—but not me. It actually had the sound of my dad's voice, but it wasn't him either; he obviously wasn't there. The voice encouraged me to look up, then keep walking towards Elliot's Ridge. Some might say it was hypothermia speaking. Hypothermia is in fact a condition where the body loses more heat to the environment than it is generating and can be life-threatening and cause delusions. Others might say the voice was some primal, final impulse kicking in before I was going to die. While it might have been any of these, or a combination of them, I know what happened and I know what I heard—so I obeyed the voice.

Putting the little Bible back into my pocket, I lifted my head, looked to Elliot's Ridge, and started climbing. I am not exactly sure who Elliot was, but the Hebrew meaning for the name Elliot is actually the "Lord is my God."[1] The specific ridge I was staring at had been used as far back as 1900 for high country sheepherding. There are remnants of stone corrals and shelters up there that the shepherds and their sheep used to inhabit. This young sheep was certainly responding to a voice that he'd heard after screaming the word of the Lord his God, and was bolting for that high country meadow and the safety that it might hold.

Climbing, stumbling, sometimes crawling, I steadily made my way to the foot of the ridge and the glacier that seemed to be a natural bridge to the top. I was so close. Clawing, scratching, and digging, I made my way to the top edge of the ridge. It wasn't pretty, but I made it. Shirt ripped, pants muddied, kneecaps freezing

---

1. Ancestry, "Elliot."

Part II: Living Out The Text

from the ice, there I was—at the crest of Elliot's Ridge. No map, no compass, no whistle, no water bottle and no food, but, yes, I had yielded to the encouragement of a voice and made it. A twelve-year-old, his Bible, and whatever or whoever was watching me—a newfound hope had begun to flicker and was growing. It was a hope that seemed to have been fueled by screaming God's word into the atmosphere, then moving towards a destination suggested by the voice inside of me—or outside of me—I wasn't sure. I was sure however that it had spoken to me, no doubt about it.

After catching my breath, I stood upright, stumbled a bit, then gathered my bearings. Scanning the landscape, I noticed over my right shoulder a large body of water. It was Green Mountain Reservoir. I had never been so thankful for a body of water in my life. State Highway 9 runs along the eastern shoreline and, while squinting, I could make out figures of small vehicles traveling around the huge body of water many miles away. Even though the reservoir was far in the distance—there it was. Hope was now very alive and pulsating with every beat of my heart. I wasn't going to die—I knew it. I verbally thanked God for his direction and began walking downhill towards that beautiful body of water. One thing I did remember from our troop meetings was that water flows downhill and would ultimately lead you to civilization. I desperately wanted to make it back to civilization, so I started to walk downhill along a path that crossed the ridge by meandering between pastoral patches of grass and glacial snow and ice. Shepherds and sheep had undoubtedly been there recently as I could still see their tracks in the snow, mud, and grass. On the downward trek, hope was my companion.

While I don't remember the entirety of the conversation, I vividly remember the voice engaging with me again and issuing to me what I would label as a "call." It was a call that meant that I too was going to be a shepherd. Not a shepherd of woolen sheep like the ones that grazed up there on Elliot's Ridge, but human ones. In my twelve-year-old mind, I didn't know everything that type of call actually entailed, but I was certain that I would be in the ministry—whatever that meant. Over the ensuing decades, I would walk with the Great Shepherd and he would teach and inform me that I would live by the power of God's word; that I would lead his people; that I would live in community with his people; and that I would do these things for the rest of my life.

This pastoral conversation lasted for several hours as I traversed the grass and snow, ultimately ending at a trailhead that had a sign with an arrow pointing to the parking lot where we had parked our vehicle on the first day. Much had transpired since then. I followed the arrow to the parking lot, ultimately to be found by a family from Texas who were four-wheeling and enjoying the Rockies. The peanut butter and jelly sandwich that they fed me while I told them my story was the best PB&J I have ever had. Those kind people then took me to a rancher's house, who fed me the best steak I have ever had before or since while I shared my story. Between bites of steak, I called my parents, who then called search and rescue, an amazing army of mountaineers who came and rescued my buddies who were still lost. Ultimately, everyone was safe and had their own stories to tell.

On a Sunday very soon after my wilderness experience, in a sermon at First Baptist Church, Pastor Burton Murdock spoke directly to me from the pulpit. He spoke of my miraculous rescue and of the fact that I had undoubtedly met God face to face. Affirming that I had certainly been called into the ministry in a special way, his thirty-minute sermon went by in what felt like a minute. It was as if he and I were the only ones in the sanctuary that day. Heaven seemed to have pushed pause for everyone else while an old minister lent his voice to God and instructed a young one about how he should live life in preparation to use his voice for Christ. That Sunday confirmed what has now been repeatedly affirmed: that what I heard and experienced on Elliot's Ridge as a scared to death twelve-year-old was orchestrated by God. Faithful to his word, he has now used my voice to proclaim his voice in various pulpits, nations, and contexts for over forty years. He said that he would do so in 1974 as together we traversed a high-country pasture, Shepherd and sheep.

Part II: Living Out The Text

FROM THIS LIFE-ALTERING EXPERIENCE, I WILL ALWAYS REMEMBER THAT...

God speaks.

The Bible is full of passages where God interacts with men and women verbally. This speaking may be something that they hear externally (this seems to be far less frequent), or internally (but not them), as in my case. Regardless, if it is from God, the voice, impression, thought, dream, vision, or however the message might come will always line up with the truth of the Bible. The voice that spoke to me certainly came to me and was supported by Scripture, my own experience, and a trusted pastoral voice.

When we speak what God speaks, faith is kindled.

Without a doubt, the little brown Bible in my pocket saved my life. As a sixty-two-year-old, I am more convinced of this than ever. I believe that proclaiming the word of God into the atmosphere as I knew I was going to die saved my life. Had I not had the word, I would have perished. One of my favorite verses has become Rom 10:17, "Consequently, faith comes from hearing the message, and the message is heard through the word about Christ." As I flipped through the verses in my Bible, the truths became not just some metaphysical, spiritual, sometime in the future truth, but right now truth. The hearing of myself speaking biblical truth, then it echoing back to me, was reality. Faith certainly came from hearing. It is his word, so we are to speak it as such. It's not something to be used selfishly for personal gain, but for Christ-centered faith and faithfulness.

It is valuable to always take God's word with you.

As I said in the above section, I have no doubt that I would have died if I had not had my little brown Bible with me. The verses highlighted by my dad brought life to me that day and have continued to do so. So, the simplest lesson to be learned is that it will serve you well to have a Bible with you, either physically or an electronic version. Over the last fifty years, I have learned many more verses than I read in my Bible that day, and I speak them when needed. I have memorized them and continue to memorize more and add them to my arsenal. That is because I know that difficulty, depression, despondency, sickness, fear, and danger will stalk me. But the lesson that I learned as a lost young boy has stayed with me and sustained me for over half a century: keep a Bible close to you—near your heart, as mine was in my shirt pocket. If you don't have a Bible close (and even if you do), memorize as much Scripture as possible so that you can recall it and speak truth into the atmosphere. Two of my favorite verses are "I have hidden your word in my heart that I might not sin against you" (Ps 119:11) and "But we have the mind of Christ" (1 Cor 2:16b).

Remember that wisdom contained in the Bible can and will keep you from making mistakes and, if you do make them, it will offer grace and help to see the situation redeemed. You can literally have Jesus think his thoughts through you. His word in you gives you the ability to think like him, and he is victorious in our lostness and will lead us towards safety and life.

6

Jesse's Story

> "You do not want to leave too, do you?" Jesus asked the Twelve. Simon Peter answered him, "Lord, to whom shall we go? You have the words of eternal life. We have come to believe and to know that you are the Holy One of God." —John 6:67–69

I don't remember a time before Jesus, nor a distinct moment of surrendering my life to him. I grew up in Upstate New York as the youngest of three brothers in a supportive and loving family. My parents had us close together, with my oldest brother Joe being two years older than me and my middle brother Jason one year older. My parents set an example of good lives with honest work, generosity towards others, and continual encouragement for my brothers and me in whatever we were interested in. We were regular churchgoers, and my parents were involved when we were young. They served in different roles, and my brothers and I attended the kids' classes (which often consisted just of us three). God was a part of our weekly lives, but not necessarily a point of teaching at home. But something clicked for me, more so than for most people I knew. Like the verse above, I accepted that God was real, Jesus was the source of eternal life, and he needed to be the foundation of my life. This belief wasn't a loud, passionate exclamation in my heart nor was it a nonchalant, emotionless statement. Honestly, it has always felt like a simple, firm conviction: "This is it. Jesus deserves my everything."

I can't point to a single event that defined my relationship with Jesus. Looking back, it feels more like a gradual, continual walk deeper with God. There was never a time I wasn't aware of him or doubted that he was with me. It is amazing to hear others' stories of radically meeting Jesus, being delivered from addiction, depression, and other hopeless situations, but I believe we also see his grace in stories like mine: God's presence sustaining faith throughout life. That being said, there have been several seasons God used to shape my relationship with him.

EARLY YEARS

I loved my comic book Bible. It was one of my go-to books throughout my elementary career. I would read it in the car and before I went to bed. I was fascinated by the stories throughout Scripture, especially hearing that these were *true*. I can still picture its pages in my mind, and, in all seriousness, attribute much of my foundational understanding of the Bible to those years. God used that simple book to lay the groundwork for grasping main characters in biblical history, their chronology, and, ultimately, how the entirety of the text culminates in Jesus.

It was also in this time that I first felt called to ministry. Again, I don't remember a moment that God spoke to me or even a word from a leader or anything like that. Similar to my original statement, I saw that faith in Christ was the most important thing in life. With that in mind, I was drawn to stories of missionaries and pastors, devouring book after book on figures like Charles Finney, Samuel Morris, Nate Saint, and Sojourner Truth. I loved their stories and wanted to live my own for Jesus. My school had a graduation ceremony for fifth graders moving to the middle school. Every student was asked to share what they wanted to be when they grew up. Young Jesse's response: "I want to be a missionary of God." That dream to serve God shifted over the years but never left.

Part II: Living Out The Text

MIDDLE AND HIGH SCHOOL

I know many Christians who came to a defining moment in their faith when they moved out of their parents' house. All of a sudden, following and prioritizing Jesus was their choice, not their family's. This is a time when the faith becomes their own or it fades into a childhood memory. My defining moment came earlier.

We had been attending a smaller church in town with a largely older population. I was the only one in the children's class by the time I got to middle school. Joe and Jason had graduated to the adult service, so I had the teacher's undivided attention. There wasn't a youth group for the older kids at that point either. Don't get me wrong, I have many warm memories of the church and truly enjoyed going. However, the demographics became a point of concern for my mom. Being the age that I was, I didn't understand all the dynamics at work nor my parents' opinions, but, in short, my mom wanted to go to a larger church in town (which meant over one hundred people on a Sunday) that had a youth group while my dad wanted to stay at the current church. At the end of the day, my mom, brothers, and I went to the new church. My dad largely stopped going. In all honesty, I was furious at first because I loved the old church so much—enough so that I told my mom I would go back to it when I turned sixteen and got my license—but it was a change that would profoundly impact my spiritual development.

My brothers and I attended the youth group together for the first few years, going to the weekly meetings and conferences. We actually had ten to fifteen other people our age in the group, and the ministry opened the church gym for a weekly hangout on Friday nights that brought in well over a hundred youth from the area. I gradually found my place there, was baptized, attended a summer intern program, read through the Bible for the first time, and, when I turned sixteen, did not follow through on my threat. The church had become home, and I had amazing leaders and mentors to do life with.

I became especially close with Pastor Brian, the lead pastor, Kathy, my youth pastor, and an older couple in the church named

Renny and Donna. The church hired me part-time to help with odds and ends of things (painting, lawn care, organizing storage areas, making coffee, preaching to the youth, crawling beneath the stage to ignite insecticide foggers, etc.). Pastor Brian introduced me to pastoral ministry and leading a church. I spent many afternoons and meals with Kathy's family and learned a lot from her during my several years of working at the church. We even worked out a program during my senior year (at a public school) so that I could be at the church several days a week for credit.

Renny and Donna hired me every summer to work in their garden. Although they had a home in town, their backyard was an amazing tapestry of flowers, herbs, trees, bushes, vegetables, and fruit. They even had a small greenhouse. They paid me far too generously and mandated that I take a break every hour, often accompanied by ice cream, pastries, and coffee. Renny and I would talk while we worked, and I would listen to his stories during our breaks. It wasn't a structured discipleship program, but I think following Jesus needs to be grounded in that type of relationship and friendship. Living in the text is much more than academically studying a book. It means being an involved member of God's family. I learned much about following Jesus during my time with these people, and I know I wouldn't be the man I am today without that season.

I continued to feel called to the ministry throughout my middle and high school years. No one in my family had been in the ministry vocationally: no preachers, pastors, or missionaries. But the call was mine. It became even more real in high school. Both of my brothers stopped going to church. I am grateful that my dad never said anything negative about the church and always supported what I felt called to, but the option was clearly there to stay home. When Sundays came around, it was just my mom and me going out the door in the morning. My mom was also a constant spiritual encouragement, always praying for and with us. We would often see her Bible and other books on prayer sitting in the living room, signs she had already been with Jesus before we were awake. On that note, I am convinced that there are countless

Part II: Living Out The Text

Christians who have been sustained by the faith of praying moms. They truly take part in the unseen work of the kingdom, and I know I've always been covered with a mother's faithful prayers.

That being said, I still had a decision to make for myself. It wasn't my parents' or brothers' decision, but mine. It was my choice to prioritize and follow Jesus, no one else's. And, by the grace of God alone, I did. "Lord, to whom shall we go? You have the words of eternal life."

COLLEGE

Much to the chagrin of my family, church, and friends, I decided not to attend a small Bible college two hours from my hometown in New York. Instead, I enrolled at Oral Roberts University (ORU) ... in Tulsa ... Oklahoma ... twenty hours away. It didn't make sense. I was spending more money to be farther away from home and my church where I thought I was going to work. It was also a four-year degree rather than the two I had planned on. However, God spoke to me through a series of events that drastically changed my five-year plan and the course of my young adult life.

These changes did not occur all at once. God directed me over six years at ORU in small decisions that led to a greater shift in my life. Various people, programs, and opportunities became magnets that drew me in slightly new directions. Among these, the most influential were the Chaplain Program, becoming a teaching assistant to one Dr. Voth (this name probably sounds familiar to you), and joining a program called Prayer Movement where I met a girl named Hannah.

The Chaplain Program

The Chaplain Program was a leadership position for the dorms at ORU. Chaplains served alongside the resident advisors (RAs). Whereas RAs handled official business like enforcing curfews, making sure rooms were cleaned, and requesting maintenance, chaplains were available for spiritual encouragement and community. For example, I led a weekly devotional time, met with my guys one-on-one, and planned regular times to hang out. There were many fun memories, and a lot of hard moments. Like I said earlier in this chapter, college tends to be a time where faith is tested, not to mention the continual drama found in romantic pursuits. Both were frequent points of prayer and counsel.

I was a chaplain for two years on freshman floors before becoming the graduate assistant for the program. At that point, I helped oversee the program as a whole, being a part of the team that organized the chaplain meetings, trainings, and retreats. Long story short, I loved being in a community that was focused on encouraging others to draw close to Jesus. It reinforced my desire and confidence to be in full-time ministry. And, naturally, matured me in the practical experience of leading, communicating, and organizing a multi-tiered program. I had great leaders to learn from, Augustine and Allie Mendoza, and I had no idea how much this time would impact my readiness for the next season.

Being a Teaching Assistant to Dr. Voth

Alongside the Chaplain Program, I became a teaching assistant for one Dr. Jeff Voth. Initially, I intended to work with him in one class for one semester. That expanded to four years of courses at ORU, followed by four more years (and counting) working together in the local church and on several books.

I just wanted to help in one class. I felt peace about that, but God turned that one step into much more. I gained a lot of experience in public speaking and working with students, but more formative has been my relationship with Jeff. There was work to do, classes to teach, assignments to grade, and papers to write, but I learned by simply doing life with him and watching. One of the greatest pieces of advice I received in college was "If you're not sure what God's vision for you is yet, serve someone else's." I knew I was called to ministry in some capacity, but I recognized I had an opportunity to serve and learn from someone who had gone

Part II: Living Out The Text

before me. Over time, watching became doing, following became leading, and my professor became a mentor and friend. My wife Hannah and I often take a step back and recognize that Jeff and his wife Lori have been foundational points of wisdom and growth in our young adult lives, more so than we probably realize in the moment. Speaking of my wife . . .

Prayer Movement and Meeting Hannah

One of my favorite groups I was involved with was Prayer Movement at ORU. This included hour-and-a-half sets in which students led prayer and worship in one of the auditoriums at the school. Other students were welcome to join in. The sets consisted of a worship team and prayer team that worked together to facilitate the time. The worship leader and prayer leader organized the set with Scripture readings, songs, prayer topics, and similar details. I am grateful for my two years in the program as it showed me the beauty and discipline of praying with one another. An hour and a half can feel like a long time, but it was a refreshing part of my rhythm to sit in God's presence, worship, and pray with brothers and sisters.

I was assigned as an assistant prayer leader my second year in the program. However, a prayer leader on a different set dropped out and I was asked to take his position. It worked with my schedule, and I said yes. The first step after this was to meet the worship leader I would be working with, a girl named Hannah. I didn't know her, and we were in different majors so I don't think I ever would have if not for Prayer Movement. We led the set that year and got to know each other through leading. I really enjoyed being with her. We remained friends the next couple years at college, getting together every so often to catch up, talk about future plans and dreams, and even give relationship advice at times. She was the person I could talk to the longest, you know the type of conversations that last hours but fly by. I loved her sense of humor, how she thought of the world, and her heart for worship. She also happened to be beautiful and one of the kindest people I had ever met. It was easy to be ourselves with each other, which made every other aspect better. In short, we were the quintessential rom-com relationship: two friends that the audience knows should be together, but they don't realize it until the season finale.

For us, that was a conversation on our graduation day. A very nervous Jesse got up the courage to risk his friendship for something so much more. Heart pounding, I confessed my feelings for her and prayed for the best. The best has been better than I could have hoped for. Hannah is my best friend, adventure partner, resting place, and God's greatest gift apart from Jesus. We still have long conversations, talk about future plans and dreams, and give relationship advice (I guess you could call it that. We talk about ours.) I've gotten the privilege to laugh with her, look at the world together, and worship God alongside her. I still find her incredibly beautiful and see Christ's kindness expressed through her in so many ways. She helps me be the version of myself that God created me to be. She is my wife and the amazing mother to our son. She, and our life together, is so much more than I expected when I agreed to lead the prayer set all those years ago.

LIVING IN THE TEXT TAKEAWAYS

So, what does all of this have to do with living in the text? Everything.

As a child, I learned to love the word.

Wherever we are at, however old we are, whatever life looks like, we need to dive into the word. The Bible is God's revealed wisdom, and our interactions with him through the word form the foundation of all we do and all we are. Jesus stated at the end of the Sermon on the Mount, "Therefore everyone who hears these words of mine and puts them into practice is like a wise man who built his house on the rock."[1] My studies with my comic book Bible

---

1. Matt 7:24.

started my lifelong passion to be in the word. Even if you came to Jesus later in life or haven't dedicated time to Scripture, don't think less of yourself or your "lack." The Holy Spirit meets us where we are at and helps us grow as we spend time with him, with others, and with his word.

As a teen, I learned the value of personal commitment and community.

By the Spirit, I made the decision to follow Jesus *for* myself, but I also learned that life in Jesus is not just *by* myself. We follow Jesus, not anyone else. As we follow him, God gives us his family of believers. We are united with one another in a more real way than our biological families: we are united in the blood of Christ. It is easy to neglect either of these facets of life in Jesus, but we need both. You are God's son or daughter if you have submitted to Jesus. You are responsible to continually remain in him and act in response to his word and leading. No one can do it for you. However, you need to be an active member of the family of God: knowing, loving, serving, supporting, and leaning on the church. As we stated in chapter 3, the Bible is communal, and our lives were made to be, as well.

As a young adult, I learned to take one step at a time.

In each of my decisions—going to ORU, being a chaplain, becoming a teaching assistant, and joining Prayer Movement—I did not know all that would happen as a result. I simply felt peace in the moment about each. Living in the text is much more than studying a book. It is knowing the voice of Jesus. It is understanding that this faith is an interactive relationship of love and submission to a heavenly Father who still speaks. Your job is not to have all the right answers or to know every step that you will ever take. Your job is to be obedient with what God has commanded you to do today. There will be specific steps and actions to follow, but Jesus instructed us with two foundational commands of our lives: "'Love the Lord your God with all your heart and with all your soul and with all your mind.' This is the first and greatest commandment. And the second is like it: 'Love your neighbor as yourself.'"[2]

How do you live in the text? It can be intimidating to consider the answer since it impacts every aspect of life. Take it slow. Be present in the moment. Be obedient in the small areas. Learn to enjoy God's presence and love your neighbor. Living in the text is a lifelong journey with Jesus. Above all, remember that he has already done it all. Scripture tells us that he who began a good work in you will carry it on to completion (Phil 1:6). As you walk with him, you will look back after days, weeks, months, and years to see the amazing ways he has guided your life and brought you closer to him.

---

2. Matt 22:37–39.

PART III

How to Live in the Text

They devoted themselves to the apostles' teaching and to fellowship, to the breaking of bread and to prayer. —ACTS 2:42

We've discussed why living in the text is needed in the world and its challenges. We've shared what the story of the text is and what it looks like to live in HIStory. Now what? How do I actually live in the text? We're glad you asked.

Like the passage above, we must be devoted to teaching, fellowship, the breaking of bread, and prayer. It encompasses all we say and all we do. It requires intentionality, listening, and dependence on the Spirit. Jesus often compared the word of God to a seed being planted. Because of this, we've divided this section into three parts: The Bible Sown, The Bible Buried, and The Bible Harvest.

Sowing: How do we interact with the word as a community? We offer three facets in response to this question: embody, share, and create. Christ reveals himself through us as individuals and as a community as we do these things in him. Sowing the word is much more than simply preaching.

Part III: How To Live In The Text

Burying: How do we interact with the word individually? This section provides a brief overview of strategies to bury the text in the soil of our lives. We are complex beings, and God interacts with each of us in a unique way. The provided list offers ways that you can invest in your time with the Spirit and his word.

Harvesting: How do we take part in the harvest of living in the text? We encourage others to grow closer to Christ. We create and support a culture of remaining in him and his word. We learn to hear God's voice to play our part in his kingdom for his glory. And we do so until Jesus returns or calls us home.

7

The Bible Sown

Nothing but fire kindles fire. —PHILLIPS BROOKS[1]

LEGENDARY THEOLOGIAN, PREACHER, AND songwriter Phillips Brooks was spot on in the above quote, wasn't he? Bottom line, you can't give what you don't have—especially in the realm of following Jesus. Echoing this sentiment, John Wesley is purported to have said that if you light yourself on fire with passion, people will come from miles to watch you burn.[2] Are you burning? We have referred to the combustible power of God's word throughout this book. His Word, Jesus, was, is, and ever will be the fruition of God's plan for all of eternity. It is a plan that is immense, full, and all encompassing, yet comprehensible enough for children to cling to in the simplicity of their faith. God himself in the Old Testament made a powerful proclamation through the prophet Isaiah in the eighth century BC, pertaining to the reverberating, incendiary effects of his word:

> As the heavens are higher than the earth, so are my
> ways higher than your ways and my thoughts than your
> thoughts. As the rain and the snow come down from

---

1. Brooks, *Lectures on Preaching*, 38.
2. Wesley, "Light Yourself on Fire."

Part III: How To Live In The Text

> heaven, and do not return to it without watering the earth and making it bud and flourish, so that it yields seed for the sower and bread for the eater, so is *my word* that goes out from my mouth: It will not return to me empty, but will accomplish what I desire and achieve the purpose for which I sent it. (Isa 55:9–11; emphasis added)

Throughout the biblical tale, the written word was repeatedly the means by which individuals, groups, and nations turned back to God. In 2 Kgs 22–23, King Josiah found the Law that had been lost and read it to the people, reestablishing the Lord as the foundation of their society. Ezra read this same word to the returned exiles in Neh 8. God's word is unchanging, unshakable, and true. Jesus is literally the embodiment, or incarnation of these words. He is the visible power of God in skin. The apostle Paul asserts,

> Therefore God exalted him to the highest place and gave him the name that is above every name, that at the name of Jesus every knee should bow, in heaven and on earth and under the earth, and every tongue acknowledge that Jesus Christ is Lord, to the glory of God the Father. (Phil 2:9–11)

As people who live in the text, we are called to follow Jesus fully, wholeheartedly, and with every ounce of our beings. That's why he spoke often about God's word—his word:

- "Heaven and earth will pass away, but my words will never pass away." (Matt 24:35)
- "The words I have spoken to you—they are full of the Spirit and life." (John 6:63)
- "My teaching is not my own. It comes from the one who sent me." (John 7:16)
- "Sanctify them by the truth; your word is truth." (John 17:17)
- "They were amazed at his teaching, because his words had authority." (Luke 4:32)

THE WORN SPOT

As we discussed in chapter 4, the Bible is the word of God. It is the written word and the living word. The power of the word in the life of the believer and the communities that bear his name is immeasurable and unfathomable; however, some of the effects can actually be seen in this real time, real world, through the time-tested processes of preaching, praying, teaching, discussing, and living the text of the word. We like to call this the *practical process* of living in the text. I (Jeff) will never forget something that caught my attention one Wednesday evening as I sat in the front row of our sanctuary, preparing to pray. As I bowed my head, my eyes fixed upon something on the floor, just to the right of the pulpit. In my curiosity, I walked up the three steps to the stage and saw something that wasn't only to the right of the pulpit, but also to the left and behind. It was a circle about six feet across and three feet wide—a place where the lacquer had worn off the wooden planks of the stage.

Over years of preaching and teaching the word from that very spot, the floor had been worn down. We had preached sermons, taught classes, had conferences, and conducted weddings and funerals from that very spot, always pointing somehow to the word. For hours upon countless hours, myself and others had verbally sown God's word in many different contexts. Some of them were learning environments, sometimes the setting was funny, sometimes celebratory, and sometimes grieving. The common denominator was always the word—the living text. Along with all the living followers of Jesus and the great cloud of witnesses who have gone before us, we have sown the word; and our Jesus focused, Bible based community in our little corner of the world has been forever changed. "Sowing the word" contains vast depths and heights in walking with Jesus, but we believe we must take part in three connected rhythms to live in the text: embodying the word, sharing the word, and creating with the word.

Part III: How To Live In The Text

EMBODY THE WORD

When discussing sowing the word, we would be remiss not to mention Billy Graham.

> Graham preached the gospel to some 215 million people who attended one or more of his more than 400 Crusades, simulcasts and evangelistic rallies in more than 185 countries and territories. He reached millions more through TV, video, film, the internet and 34 books.[3]

Billy Graham preached the good news of Jesus Christ. However, his ministry was far more than speaking. Graham embodied the truth of Jesus and the Bible in every area of life. He held desegregated crusades in the 1950s, welcomed hippies into the family of faith when many Christians rejected those of the Jesus Revolution, and supported Christian music expanding into new genres that more traditional believers were wary of.[4] He prayed with twelve different presidents of both political parties while rejecting the idea that he should run for office himself.[5] He never took part in scandal or disgrace throughout his entire ministry.[6] He didn't just preach the word, he embodied it.

We no longer live, but Christ lives in us. If this is true, he is the lens through which every facet of our being shines: our integrity, finances, politics, disciplines, and social efforts. We sow the good news of Jesus Christ through our lives, not just syllables on our lips or letters typed on a page. Although we introduced this idea in two paragraphs, it encompasses a process that never ends. This entails far more than taking a step back, acknowledging changes you need to make, and proceeding accordingly. Again, Christ demands our lives *daily*. Like the apostle Paul, do not consider yourself yet arrived.[7] Jesus is Lord over every area of our lives for all of our lives. It requires continual interaction with him, his word, and his people.

3. Billy Graham Evangelistic Association, "Billy Graham, Evangelist."
4. Blumhofer, *Songs I Love to Sing*, 4.
5. Billy Graham Evangelistic Association, "Billy Graham: Pastor."
6. Jefferson, "Remembering the Rev. Billy Graham."
7. Phil 3:12–14.

Some of this change is the result of intentional effort: I recognize the need for change in an area, devote this area to Jesus, and make changes empowered by the Spirit to live like him. Some changes, indeed most, come gradually when we aren't thinking about them. As we spend time with Jesus, his word, and his people, we will naturally look more and more like him. He draws us to himself and lives through us.

Sowing the Bible through embodying the word is the foundation of all other efforts. Jesus instructed his listeners to take the speck out of their eye first before helping others. He is not interested in us just as his tools to reach the world. That would make us only means to an end. Realize that you are an end, in and of yourself, to Jesus. He cares for you and wants to express his life fully through you completely. As we do this together, his light shines all the clearer to the world.

SHARE THE WORD

One hundred years ago, missionaries moved to the Central African Republic to share the gospel of Jesus Christ. They bought one-way tickets and shipped their belongings in caskets. They planned to live and die in Africa.[8] The apostle Paul stated in Acts 20:24, "However, I consider my life worth nothing to me; my only aim is to finish the race and complete the task the Lord Jesus has given me—the task of testifying to the good news of God's grace." The Christian movement has progressed through generations because believers shared the good news of Jesus Christ with others, regardless of danger and persecution. If you have called on the name of Jesus, it is because someone told someone who told someone who told someone who told someone (for almost two thousand years) who told you.

Jesus stated in Matt 28:18–20,

> All authority in heaven and on earth has been given to me. Therefore go and make disciples of all nations,

---

8. *Chicago Tribune*, "Missionaries Facing World."

Part III: How To Live In The Text

baptizing them in the name of the Father and of the Son and of the Holy Spirit, and teaching them to obey everything I have commanded you. And surely I am with you always, to the very end of the age.

This passage is called the Great Commission. Jesus' followers have been commissioned with this call: spread the news and make disciples. Embodying the word is the foundation of the Christian life, but we cannot truly embody the word if we do not share it. Those who truly embody the word share it, and those who truly share the word embody it.

So what do we share?

1. All have sinned and fall short of the glory of God (Rom 3:23).
2. God became man in Jesus and took the punishment of sin on himself (Isa 53:5–6).
3. All who accept Jesus as Lord and repent of their sins will be forgiven (John 3:16–18).
4. Jesus lives eternally in and through those who receive him (Gal 2:20).

Become an expert in sharing the story of Jesus. Learn to hear God's voice, follow his leading, and share his hope, light, and life with those you come in contact with. Scripture tells us that God draws people to himself (John 6:44). Our role as Christians is to pray and speak, trusting that God will reveal himself even to the most unlikely of people. Sow the Bible through sharing the word.

CREATE WITH THE WORD

The great Reformer Martin Luther understood how profound an impact the Bible could have upon culture, so much so that he endeavored to write and/or copy culturally accepted musical scores and merge them with scriptural truths. Especially concerned with how music affected the next generation, he stated that he

> should like young people, who in any case should and must be instructed in music and in other proper arts, to have at their disposal something which will rid their minds of lascivious and sensual songs, and teach them instead something wholesome, and in their way they may become acquitted with goodness in a joyous manner, as befits the young.[9]

No doubt Luther understood the power of the word, synthesized with music, especially upon young, malleable spirits and minds. Addressing the young, he remarked,

> And you, my young friends, let this noble wholesome and cheerful creation of God be commended to you. By it you may escape shameful desires and bad company. At the same time, you may by this creation accustom yourselves to recognize and praise the Creator. Take special care to shun perverted minds who prostitute this lovely gift of nature and of art with their erotic rantings, and be quite assured that none but the devil goads them on to defy their very nature, which would and should praise God its Maker with this gift.[10]

Church worship music is still heavily influenced by younger Christians. However, regardless of age or culture, Luther explained the goal for all faith-based music:

> We intend to follow the example of the prophets and the ancient Fathers of the church, and to make a collection of a certain number of psalms for the people, so that the word of God may be kept alive in their hearts by song.[11]

Our God is a creative God. We, being made in his image, are creative beings. Living in the text should lead us to create and imagine and dream. We sow the word lastly through creativity. God delights when we use our gifts and abilities to glorify him. He

---

9. Holman, "Luther."
10. Holman, "Luther."
11. Holman, "Luther."

even anointed people in the Old Testament to be craftsmen and singers (Exod 31:1–5 and 2 Chr 20:21).

This creativity can overtly or covertly reflect Jesus. For example, *The Lion, the Witch and the Wardrobe*, in the Chronicles of Narnia, is a direct retelling of Christ's story: Aslan, the lion-King (not Mufasa) offers himself to take the punishment of Edmund, a rebellious boy. Aslan surrenders himself to the villain and her cronies, allowing them to humiliate and kill him. However, he rises from the dead and brings life to others who had been killed by the evil witch.[12] Lewis called this a "supposal," stating that the story presents a tale of what it would look like if there were another world and what Jesus would look like if he went there.[13] An overt retelling of the gospel.

J. R. R. Tolkien's Lord of the Rings series is a covert expression of Christ. Although there are biblical elements such as the battle of good versus evil, the temptation of sin, the necessity of community, and resurrection, they don't directly tell the gospel message. Both works are of the highest quality and reveal God's kingdom in unique ways. Being Christian doesn't give an excuse for subpar creations, but rather gives more reason and inspiration to create great things *with* God. One mathematician, Johannes Kepler, cited his faith as a driving force behind his work. To him, all scientific and mathematical advancements were discoveries of what God had already placed in creation. Thinkers and scientists merely thought God's thoughts after him.[14]

We sow the word by approaching our own work, arts, and hobbies through the lens of Christ. Our music, architecture, poetry, and film can and should point to Jesus. All things are held together in Jesus. Living in the text is more than living rightly and sharing news: it is living life to the *full* in him. When we do that, he will shine through our lives all the more, bringing hope, light, and life through his people.

---

12. Lewis, *Lion, the Witch and the Wardrobe*.
13. Wilson, "Why Narnia Isn't Allegorical."
14. Travis, *Thinking God's Thoughts*, 6.

SUMMARY POINTS

- The Bible repeatedly shows God using his word to realign his people with his will. King Josiah and Ezra both were pivotal characters who presented the Law to the people as a form of recommitment to the Lord. The word fulfills the same role in our life today: realignment, refinement, and empowerment.
- We live in the text by sowing the word in our lives and our communities. We sow the word when we take part in three rhythms:

  1. *Embody the Word:* We allow the Holy Spirit to shape us to be like Christ. The word molds every aspect of our lives, including our finances, disciplines, priorities, speech, social interactions, and politics. We first sow the word in our lives that we may accurately reflect the truth of the word. Embodying the word requires a daily dependence on the Holy Spirit. We never arrive but continually walk in and with Jesus.

  2. *Share the Word:* We tell the story of Jesus—why he came, how he lived, what he taught, how he was raised to life, and how we can know and live in him. Jesus gave his disciples the Great Commission to go into all the world to make disciples. If you know Jesus, it is because a chain of believers going all the way back to the disciples faithfully told Christ's story to others. By his Spirit, we should be about the same work, telling his story to family members, friends, neighbors, and coworkers.

  3. *Create with the Word:* Our God is a creative God, and we are creative beings. His life and word should permeate all we do and all we create. Our songs, art, and culture should flow from and to Jesus. Christianity isn't a lifeless, stuffy existence. It is living life to the full, and that includes our creativity and imaginations. We have more reason than any to produce excellent and inspiring work with our hands and minds.

Part III: How To Live In The Text

- When we take part in these rhythms, the Spirit sows his word in and through our lives.

8

The Bible Buried

WHO IS DOING IT RIGHT?

CHARITY BEGINS EVERY DAY the same way: twenty minutes with her Bible, a journal, and a cup of coffee. She is working through a Bible reading plan and usually ends her time by praying over her family, responsibilities, and needs that she's aware of. She feels she does a good job of prioritizing this time.

Sam enjoys reading large portions of Scripture regularly, entire books of the Bible if possible. He takes Sunday afternoon as his Sabbath and dives into a text then. Then, he reflects on what he read for the rest of the week. This doesn't always mean he is in the Bible every day, though he has a rhythm of prayer and worship during the work week.

Lately, Hope has been leaning into silence and listening in her time with Jesus. She will read a psalm or a smaller portion of Scripture and reflect on it. She asks God to speak to her and spends the majority of her time in silence. Her time varies some, usually from five to thirty minutes, but she feels refreshed and grounded after her prayer.

Who is living in the text correctly? Who is doing it right?

That, my friends, is the wrong question. The easiest instruction we could give would be a set schedule and formula for Bible reading and prayer: wake up at this time, read this much, pray this

Part III: How To Live In The Text

prayer, see your life transformed. Although well meaning, that would be misguided. *What* you do is not as important as *how* you do it. Let me explain.

Spiritual disciplines are a wonderful gift, but they, like Scripture, are a means to an end: to live in and with Jesus. Schedules, rhythms, traditions, and rituals can be incredibly helpful in our spiritual lives, but only if they are submitted to Christ. God has a unique relationship with each of his children. In his book *Emotionally Healthy Discipleship* Peter Scazzero states, "While Jesus did teach large groups, he knew that one size did not fit all when it came to discipleship. He chose just twelve individuals from the multitudes and customized their training and discipleship to meet their unique needs."[1] Jesus has a special way that he wants to be with you.

What we are saying is that how we interact with Jesus through the Bible, prayer, and other disciplines is itself an interaction with Jesus. What we do, what we read, how we pray, and every other detail of our "devotions" should be guided by him. We live in the text by living in him.

This chapter is a resource, providing you with tools in your spiritual life. It consists of explanations and examples of several disciplines you can use in your time with Jesus: memorization, *lectio divina*, silence, fasting, and different reading methods. Scripture and the historic church show us that these are effective means to bury the word in our lives so that it takes root and brings forth Christ's life in us. Before we start, a few points for context. We are to live in the text:

1. *Without Ceasing:* In 1 Thess 5:17 (ESV) Paul states, "pray without ceasing." We are constantly dependent on the Holy Spirit. Apart from Jesus, we can do no good thing. Although we aren't suggesting a set, daily schedule, we need Jesus every day. We need to be in prayer, aware of his presence, listening for his voice, and reflecting his life by his Spirit. These apply in every season of life.

---

1. Scazzero, *Emotionally Healthy Discipleship*, 24.

2. *Within Community:* You should discuss what you feel God leading you in with trusted believers. If you are a part of a local church, pay attention to opportunities to learn and engage with the body, such as prayer meetings and Bible studies. If God called you there, submit to the vision of the house and join in as you are able. If you are not a part of a local church, prayerfully join one. We need each other.

3. *According to Scripture:* Connected to the former point, the Spirit will never lead you to a practice or belief that contradicts his word. The Bible and the community of believers are safeguards for us. Sometimes we miss what God was saying, but Scripture is the rule to which we are to measure all things.

MEMORIZATION

> *Bible memorization* is absolutely fundamental to spiritual formation. If I had to—and of course, I don't have to—choose among all the disciplines of the spiritual life and take only one, I would choose Bible memorization. . . . Bible memorization is a fundamental way of filling our minds with what they need. "Do not let this Book of the Law depart from your mouth" (Josh. 1:8). That is where we need it! In our mouths. How did it get in your mouth? Memorization.[2]

Many people we speak with assume that memorizing Scripture is a difficult task meant for the spiritually elite or just those in ministry. However, it is a gift meant for every believer. The Lord repeatedly encouraged his people to discuss his word with their families (Deut 6:4–8) and to meditate on the Law (Josh 1:6–9). When Jesus was tempted in the wilderness, he responded with Scripture (Matt 4). The apostle Paul wrote that the word of God is the sword of the Spirit (Eph 6:17). There is power in the word.

Memorizing does come easier to some than to others, but it is worth the effort for everyone. Our church, Church 3434, went through a six-month series in the book of Psalms. To engage the

---

2. Willard, "Spiritual Formation."

Part III: How To Live In The Text

congregation in our process, we invited members to memorize the psalms we would be preaching on. They were given several weeks to prepare. Then, every sermon began with our members reciting the chapter to the congregation. We had almost forty different people join in during the series. It was hard for some, and we had a copy of the passage on hand if needed. For many, it was the first time they had ever committed a chapter to memory. We had children, youth, spouses, and elders take part.

We share this to say that Bible memorization can be challenging, but it is possible. It is a process, but it is worth it. It is a discipline, but God uses it to slow us down and speak to our hearts.

Bible Memorization Example

If you haven't memorized the Bible before, start small. Pick a verse that is encouraging or challenging. Some of the first verses we memorized are Luke 9:23, Acts 20:24, Gal 2:20, and 2 Cor 5:17.

If you would like to challenge yourself, choose a chapter to memorize. It could even be a part of a book that you'd like to expand into. Some helpful rhythms include listening to the passage, writing it down and putting it in a place you will see it often, and reciting it one line at a time, adding verses as you grow more familiar with the preceding ones. Begin and end with prayer, asking Jesus to be with you, guide you, and speak to you through his word.

LECTIO DIVINA

Lectio divina means "divine reading." It is Latin, but, for those wary of church history, do not be afraid. Christians have been practicing this method of reading and prayer since the third century, several hundred years before any denominational splits in the church. *Lectio divina* is a slow-paced, prayerful reflection on a passage of Scripture. Listening for God's guidance is a foundational aspect of this practice. One author states that the monks who practiced this "listened not so much to understand the text, not to conceptualize or analyze it, but just to hear it. And to hear it without any preconceived purpose of what they were going to do with it."[3]

Rather than Bible "study," *lectio divina* is a way we listen for God's voice through the lens of the Bible. We ask him to speak through a verse, word, or idea. We slow down to breathe in his presence and reflect on his truth.

Lectio Divina Example

J. I. Packer, a theologian and one of the editors on the English Standard Version, gives this outline of *lectio divina*:

> *Silencio* (Silence) Find a quiet spot and settle down, relax. Open yourself to the Holy Spirit.
>
> *Lectio* (Reading) Slowly read the text aloud, in a low voice. There is no hurry, so do not try to rush through.
>
> *Meditatio* (Meditation) When you come to a word or phrase that seems to speak to you, repeat it slowly again and again. Reflect on its meaning. Let the text sink deep into your heart. You may even wish to imagine in your mind's eye the event or scene.
>
> *Oratio* (Praying) What does God seem to be saying to you? How does your heart respond? Open your heart to God in whatever way is appropriate—pain, joy, gratitude, confession, commitment, etc. Give honest expression to your thoughts, feelings and desires before God.
>
> *Contemplatio* (Resting) Quietly sit in God's presence, rest in his arms. He may or may not give further insight.[4]

Lectio divina does not remove our responsibility to know the word, its context, and intended meaning, but it is a good reminder that our interaction with Christ is more than studying a textbook.

---

3. Packer, "Overview," 3.
4. Packer, "Overview," 5.

Part III: How To Live In The Text

SILENCE

I (Jesse) once went on a spiritual retreat with some friends to the hills of Arkansas. The monastery we stayed at was in the middle of nowhere. It was quiet: no distant traffic, no light pollution, no cell service. Our purpose was to be with God and to hear his voice. The believers there encouraged us to embrace the quiet. We would stop speaking at 10:00 PM and wouldn't speak until breakfast the next morning. A bell would ring fifteen minutes before any service, beginning a time of silence to prepare for our time together. It was *intentional*.

There is a difference between intentional silence and a lack of noise. The discipline of silence is dedicated time apart from distractions to focus on being with God. We set our hearts on him and take our eyes off ourselves or the circumstances around us. Peter Scazzero lists four reasons why silence is transformative in our relationship with Jesus:

1. In silence we let go, surrendering our will to God's will.
2. In silence we let go of our agendas, allowing communion with God to become the core of our lives.
3. In silence we let go, allowing God to deeply transform us.
4. In silence we let go, opening ourselves to hear God speak.[5]

Silence is a great practice to begin your devotional time or to re-center in the middle of a busy day. It can be a challenge at first. We live in a culture designed to catch and keep our attention. Have grace for yourself but try to challenge yourself, as well. Start with a minute of silence and build from there. When your mind starts to wander, which it will, say Jesus' name to refocus. Don't think of your prayer requests, day ahead, or things you "should" be doing instead. Just be with your Father in heaven.

---

5. Scazzero, *Emotionally Healthy Discipleship*, 54–56.

FASTING

Fasting has been applied to many areas, including social media, screens, music, and homework (an answer I [Jesse] received when I asked middle schoolers what they wanted to fast from). These can be helpful, but, in Scripture, fasting always applied to food—the deliberate abstinence of sustenance to draw near to God. Elijah, John the Baptist, and Jesus all fasted regularly. Jesus told his listeners that his followers would fast when he was no longer with them (Luke 5:35). Fasting is a very pointed discipline: we deny our flesh so that our spirits will be strengthened. More than a diet, fasting entails focusing on God in place of food and drink. It is fasting *and* praying.

The Bible gives examples of fasts being called in response to difficult circumstances and as part of the normal rhythm for individuals and groups. We can think of fasting in the same way. Many churches have set times of the year dedicated to fasting and prayer. If yours does, be intentional in joining as you are able. Some people find it helpful to incorporate fasting into their weekly rhythm, choosing a meal or entire day to fast.

Fasting costs you something: your comfort. I don't normally dream of fast food or get mesmerized by ads for donuts, but it becomes a real struggle in fasting. However, it is also an indicator of how often we give our bodies whatever they want, regardless of how healthy or unhealthy those things are. Hunger is a reminder of our need for Jesus, much more important than our need for food. If you are physically able, you could choose a meal to fast, instead spending time in prayer or worship. Or, if you would like to try a longer fast, speak with a mentor or leader about the best way to do so.

READING METHODS

Finally, there are several unique ways you can interact with God's word. These are not necessarily different disciplines, but they are different expressions of meditating on Scripture.

Part III: How To Live In The Text

Reading Large Portions

The Bible communicates God's story, but sometimes we lose sight of that overarching narrative when we focus on a single chapter at a time. Consuming larger portions of Scripture helps clarify the book's context and meaning, as well as its place in the overall story of the Bible. For example, you could read through smaller books in one sitting or dedicate a week to working through larger books like Genesis. Audio Bibles are a great tool for this as you can listen to the story as you drive or exercise.

Out Loud

> But his delight is in the law of the Lord, and in his law he meditates (*hagah*) day and night. [(Ps 1:2)]
>
> The Hebrew word *hagah*, translated "meditates" in Psalm 1, conveys the image of a person slowly, thoughtfully murmuring to themselves as they mull repeatedly over an idea. The psalmist tells us this is what the blessed person does—continuously recites the Torah aloud.[6]

Speaking God's word engages our minds, mouths, ears, and hearts. We think of the word, speak the word, hear the word, and abide in the word. It helps us focus as, practically, reading something out loud keeps our minds present rather than wandering. This is a small shift that can make a large impact on your presentness with Jesus in the word.

In Community

As we stated earlier, the Bible is a communal book. One way to interact with it is to simply read it out loud in a group. It is beneficial both to the readers speaking the word and the group listening to the word. Our church dedicated several mid-week services to

---

6. Ponder, "Literature for a Lifetime Show Notes." Discussed in the podcast by Mackie et al., "Literature for a Lifetime," 37:02–38:10.

reading the Gospel of Mark. We were about to start a series going through Mark and wanted us as a community to prepare for the walkthrough. For five weeks in a row, we asked members to join us as we listened to the entirety of the book. We went through different versions each week, provided coffee and other drinks, and had teams of four people read the book over the group. It took an hour and a half. You could try something like this, an entire book or chapter, with other believers. The Spirit moves as we hear and speak the word with one another.

LOVE GOD, AND DO WHAT YOU WILL

Saint Augustine once said, "Love God, and do what you will."[7] This would be our encouragement as to *how* you live in the text in your regular rhythm. "Love God" is not a generic instruction or passive state of being, but an interactive and loving relationship with Jesus and his body. He will lead you in new seasons in different ways, and that leading requires absolute dependence on him. Schedules, reading plans, small groups, and anything else that gives structure to your time with Jesus can be helpful, but they can't be the foundation. Allow Jesus himself to lead you as you live in the text. Love God, and do what you will.

SUMMARY POINTS

- In our spiritual lives, *what* we do is not as important as *how* we do it. There is not a magic schedule, reading plan, prayer routine, or anything else that is the exact "right" way to spend time with Jesus. Rather, living in the text is founded upon a continual relationship and interaction with Jesus. Even how we plan our reading, praying, and anything else should be an interaction with Jesus. He has a unique way he wants to be with each one of us.

---

7. Ratcliffe, "St. Augustine."

Part III: How To Live In The Text

- Foundationally, we are to live in the text:
    1. *Without Ceasing:* We need to continually be dependent on the Spirit and his guidance.
    2. *Within Community:* God has given us his body for our good. None of this should be done in isolation.
    3. *According to Scripture:* Nothing we do should contradict the word of God. Scripture is the rule to which we measure all things.

- Some practices and disciplines that are tools to bury the word in your life include:
    1. *Bible Memorization:* Dedicating verses, chapters, and books to memory. This process slows us down and sets our hearts on God's word.
    2. *Lectio Divina:* The ancient practice of listening for God's voice through a text. It includes silence, reading, meditation, praying, and resting with the word.
    3. *Silence:* Intentionally removing distractions and noise to listen for God's voice. We surrender our time and control to be with God.
    4. *Fasting:* Abstaining from food and drink to be with Jesus. We embrace temporary discomfort to prioritize prayer and study.
    5. *Different Reading Methods:* Reading large portions of Scripture in shorter time frames, reading out loud, and reading in a community are all different ways to interact with the Bible.

- Allow Jesus to lead you as you meditate on and bury his word in your life. He will lead in different ways in different season, so we must prioritize listening to his voice.

9

The Bible Harvest

Our Christian conviction is that the Bible has both authority and relevance to a degree quite extraordinary in so ancient a book—and that the secret of both is in Jesus Christ. Indeed, we should never think of Christ and the Bible apart. "The Scriptures . . . bear witness to me," he said (John 5:39), and in so saying also bore his witness to them. This reciprocal testimony between the Living Word and the written Word is the clue to our Christian understanding of the Bible. For his testimony to it assures us of its authority, and its testimony to him of its relevance. The authority and the relevance are his. —John R. Stott[1]

MAKE DISCIPLES OF ALL NATIONS

People who are of the word and in the word stand out—that's the point. The place on the map or the date on the calendar doesn't make a difference. Jesus himself is the serpent-crushing messianic hope of the Old Testament Scripture, an actual physical presence in the New Testament Gospels, being lived out today through his redemptive presence in the body of believers—the church.

A little over two thousand years ago Jesus gave tactical directions to his disciples as to where and how the process of

---

1. Stott, "Culture and the Bible."

PART III: How To Live In The Text

permeating the world with the good news of his word was to be accomplished. The serpent was to be crushed by the resurrected seed of the woman, starting with the disciples themselves:

> Then the eleven disciples went to Galilee, to the mountain where Jesus had told them to go. When they saw him, they worshiped him; but some doubted. Then Jesus came to them and said, "All authority in heaven and on earth has been given to me. Therefore go and make disciples of all nations, baptizing them in the name of the Father and of the Son and of the Holy Spirit, and teaching them to obey everything I have commanded you. And surely I am with you always, to the very end of the age." (Matt 28:16–20)

These verses beg two questions:

1. Did they accomplish their task?
2. If not, what is yet to be done?

Let's tackle question one: Did they accomplish their task? First, we must clarify their specific task. The way we read the text is that the eleven disciples were to go and make disciples of all nations. In order to do this, we must know how many nations exist. According to WorldAtlas.com, there are 195 nations (including the Vatican and Palestine).[2] The original hearers of Jesus' message didn't have 195 nations to go to, so it is fair to say that they were commissioned by their Lord to go on his behalf to the known world, then ultimately to wherever people would be located on planet Earth. Hence, the task was to be continual. Dr. Henry Morris gives a broader context for Jesus' commission than merely the New Testament. Christ happened to be referring to many Old Testament texts here:

> "Ask of me, and I shall give thee the heathen for thine inheritance, and the uttermost parts of the earth for thy possession." (Psalm 2:8)
> This colorful and comprehensive phrase, usually translated "ends of the earth," occurs no less than thirty

---

2. Price, "How Many Countries."

times in the Old Testament and five in the New. The verse in our text is God's promise to his Son (Psalm 2:7), and it appears again and again. For example: "He shall have dominion also from sea to sea, and from the river unto the ends of the earth" (Psalm 72:8). "Now shall he be great unto the ends of the earth" (Micah 5:4); "All the ends of the world shall remember and turn unto the Lord" (Psalm 22:27).[3]

So, how did Jesus' disciples do? How has each generation thereafter done? At the risk of grossly oversimplifying two thousand years of church history, here is a summary:

- The eleven disciples and other early church leaders spread out in every direction, sharing the gospel of Jesus throughout the Roman Empire and beyond. Tradition has these followers going into Europe, Asia, and Africa, establishing bodies of believers.

- Christianity continued to be a persecuted religion under the next several emperors, until it became the official religion of the empire under Constantine. For better and worse, Christianity became popular and advantageous with tax benefits and social status.

- Believers continued to live out the Great Commission through sharing the good news of Jesus Christ to their immediate context, surrounding areas, and the world at large.

- From outside the church, our faith survived the rise and fall of empires, natural disasters, villainous tyrants, temptations of culture, and persecution through the centuries.

- From within, the church has far from a perfect history. People have often committed terrible acts in the name of Jesus. Wars, enslavement, and persecution have happened beneath the banner of faith—including crusades, inquisitions, and colonialism—though these periods do not accurately reflect the teachings and heart of God. But the word continued to

---

3. Morris, "Uttermost," paras. 1–2 (emphasis original).

go forth, and there have been countless Christ-followers who have lived and expressed his kingdom accurately to the world. The creation of hospitals and orphanages, the care of the poor and outcast, the abolition of slavery, the teaching of the inherent value of humanity, and the encouragement of literacy and learning are also fruits of the church. Most importantly, God has used his imperfect people to communicate his salvation only through Jesus Christ.

- Christianity now has a significant population on every continent in the world. It is easy to take this for granted, especially if you grew up in the West. The Bible, Christian thought, and Christian leaders have profoundly shaped nations and cultures. But take a step back: This faith began with Jesus and his immediate followers. The apostles took this news, and, through the Spirit, shared it with the world. Their actions set off a chain of events that led to now—to you knowing the story and even reading this book. The word went from Judea to Samaria to the ends of the earth.

TO THE UTTERMOST BOUNDS OF THE EARTH

What does this mean for us? The work is not finished. We are to take our place as the next generation of faithful sons and daughters who will keep going to their concentric circles: Jerusalem, Judea, Samaria, and the uttermost. When founding the university that bears his name, Oral Roberts received this vision statement from God: "Raise up your students to hear my voice, to go where my light is dim, where my voice is heard small, and my healing power is not known, even to the uttermost bounds of the earth. Their work will exceed yours, and in this I am well pleased."[4]

That is our call as Christians. We live in the text and share Christ until we're done and he ends it all, or we die—whichever comes first. Christ has bought us at a price. We are not our own, but live in, through, to, and for him.

4. Oral Roberts University, "Vision and Mission."

> For it is by grace you have been saved, through faith—and this is not from yourselves, it is the gift of God—not by works, so that no one can boast. For we are God's handiwork, created in Christ Jesus to do good works, which God prepared in advance for us to do. (Eph 2:8–10)

God has prepared good works for you to do, but you will only fulfill God's purposes as you remain in him and live in the text. There is much turmoil, worry, and distractions in the world that would numb you to the full life of Christ. Stay awake and work while it is day. Night will come when no one can work.

However, we don't work hard to earn our salvation or right standing before God in Christ. But since we have been given these things in Christ Jesus, don't we have more reason than anyone to strain forward with every fiber of our being, pouring out every ounce of our lives at the feet of Jesus? The apostle Paul wrote in Phil 3:10–14,

> I want to know Christ—yes, to know the power of his resurrection and participation in his sufferings, becoming like him in his death, and so, somehow, attaining to the resurrection from the dead. Not that I have already obtained all this, or have already arrived at my goal, but I press on to take hold of that for which Christ Jesus took hold of me. Brothers and sisters, I do not consider myself yet to have taken hold of it. But one thing I do: Forgetting what is behind and straining toward what is ahead, I press on toward the goal to win the prize for which God has called me heavenward in Christ Jesus.

We try hard for a different reason now. We exert ourselves not *for* salvation but *from* salvation. And we do so together. The world is aching for Christians to stand and show the truth and life of Christ. The harvest is plentiful. The workers are few.

We have begun working this worldview into the fabric of our church, Church 3434. Our staff provides a daily devotional to our congregation as a reminder of the passage we walked through the previous Sunday. We offer a series of spiritual disciplines to equip our people to live in the text, such as the given passage to meditate

Part III: How To Live In The Text

on, prayer exercises, and questions to discuss with their families. Our children's classes also teach the same Scripture covered in the Sunday sermon. Each lesson is tailored to the class so that the whole family learns from the same text. Lastly, we have various groups that meet regularly to discuss the passage from the week. This model is repetitive, straightforward, and grounded in the word of God. It slows us down as a community to focus on Jesus and his word.

How does God want to use you to encourage this culture of knowing his voice, remaining in Scripture, and depending on his Spirit? Invite him to transform you from the inside out. Prayerfully apply these things to your life and to your community. Be a part of a cultural shift away from the noise and into the text. Dive into being a disciple who makes disciples in Jesus, discuss the word, encourage and challenge one another, and be a part of the heavenly harvest. Live in the text.

There is not much time. We are closer now than we have ever been to standing before Jesus. Jonathan Edwards, one of the leaders of the American Great Awakening in the 1700s, wrote a series of resolutions for his life when he was around twenty years old. He perceived the value and opportunity of each second on this earth. One of his resolutions states, "Resolved, never to lose one moment of time; but improve it the most profitable way I can."[5]

Following Christ is a challenging call because it is not a one-time decision. Living in the text is a continual reliance on and remaining in Jesus. It is making the most of every moment, great and small. It isn't glamorous or "successful" in the world's eyes. Like the kingdom, it is as quiet and meek as a seed growing beneath the soil, as humble as a kind word and prayer for an enemy, and as radical as a voluntary death on a cross. However, a house's foundation can break before the unseen expansion of roots, the staunchest enemy can become a beloved brother or sister, and the tomb of death can now burst open because of the resurrection life of Christ. Living in the text is unassuming but powerful, countercultural but true, and extreme but the standard for the Christian life.

5. Edwards, "Resolutions."

Now, may the Lord bless you and keep you, and make his face shine upon you. May he silence the noise of the world and train your heart to hear his voice. May his word come alive to you like never before as you experience the everyday glory of living in Christ. May he use you to bring a harvest of new sons and daughters who walk in the freedom and power of his Spirit. We pray this in the name of Jesus, our hope and our redeemer, our faithful King who will return. Amen and a thousand more amens.

> He who testifies to these things says, "Yes, I am coming soon."
> Amen. Come, Lord Jesus.
> The grace of the Lord Jesus be with God's people. Amen.
> (Rev 22:20–21)

SUMMARY POINTS

- Jesus gave his disciples the ongoing task of the Great Commission. They were to go to their known world with his good news. Believers since that call have had the same mission.

- The disciples spread throughout the Roman Empire, establishing new bodies of believers. Christianity was a persecuted faith until Constantine made it the official religion of the empire.

- Our faith continued to expand and has endured countless external threats, including the rise and fall of nations, natural disasters, hostile leaders, compromising cultures, and persecution.

- From within, the church has weathered a checkered past: wars, enslavement, and persecution happened falsely under the banner of Christ. Many have used Jesus' name for their own gain.

- However, many Christians have accurately represented Jesus and his kingdom by caring for the poor, loving the outcast, and, most importantly, sharing the salvation found only in Jesus Christ.

Part III: How To Live In The Text

- Christianity now has a significant influence on every continent and has shaped nations and cultures for centuries. Believers were faithful over the past two thousand years to walk in the Great Commission, but the work is not finished.
- God has called us to walk in the same Commission: to go to our concentric circles, bringing the hope, light, and life of Jesus to our immediate contexts and the ends of the earth.
- He has given us good works to do (Eph 2:8–10), but we are not saved by those works. We serve Jesus *from* salvation, not *for* salvation. He has given us his Spirit to embody his life and share it with others.
- Each believer should ask Jesus to guide them in how to best use every moment for his glory. How does God want to transform your life and your community through his word?
- The call to live in the text is countercultural and extreme but is the standard for the Christian life.

Bibliography

Ancestry. "Elliot." Ancestry. Accessed Sept. 10, 2024. https://www.ancestry.com/first-name-meaning/elliot.

Athanasius. *On the Incarnation*. Translated by Penelope Lawson. Shippensburg, PA: Sea Harp, 2022.

Augustine. *The Confessions of Saint Augustine*. Translated by Edward B. Pusey. Grand Rapids: Christian Classics Ethereal Library, n.d. https://ccel.org/ccel/a/augustine/confess/cache/confess.pdf.

Billy Graham Evangelistic Association. "Billy Graham, Evangelist to the World, Dead at Age 99." Feb. 21, 2018. https://billygraham.org/story/billy-graham-evangelist-to-the-world-dead-at-age-99/.

———. "Billy Graham: Pastor to Presidents." Feb. 2, 2024. https://billygraham.org/story/billy-graham-pastor-to-presidents-2/.

Blumhofer, Edith. *Songs I Love to Sing: The Billy Graham Crusades and the Shaping of Modern Worship*. Grand Rapids: Eerdmans, 2023.

Bonhoeffer, Dietrich. *The Cost of Discipleship*. New York: Touchstone, 2018.

Brooks, Phillips. *Lectures on Preaching*. New York: Dutton, 1878.

Buechner, Frederick. *Wishful Thinking: A Theological ABC*. New York: Harper Row, 1973.

Cambridge Dictionary. "Thesis." https://dictionary.cambridge.org/us/dictionary/english/thesis.

Centers for Disease Control. "Screen Time vs. Lean Time Infographic." https://archive.cdc.gov/www_cdc_gov/nccdphp/dnpao/multimedia/infographics/getmoving.html.

Chicago Tribune. "Missionaries Facing World of New Perils." Updated Aug. 20, 2021. https://www.chicagotribune.com/2001/04/28/missionaries-facing-world-of-new-perils/.

Edwards, Jonathan. "The Resolutions of Jonathan Edwards." *Desiring God*, Dec. 30, 2006. https://www.desiringgod.org/articles/the-resolutions-of-jonathan-edwards.

Encyclopaedia Britannica. "Treaty of Versailles." Accessed Sept. 20, 2024. https://www.britannica.com/event/Treaty-of-Versailles-1919.

BIBLIOGRAPHY

Gottfried, Jeffrey. "Americans' Social Media Use." Pew Research Center, Jan. 31, 2024. https://www.pewresearch.org/internet/2024/01/31/americans-social-media-use/.

Hansel, Tim. *When I Relax I Feel Guilty*. Colorado Springs: D. C. Cook, 1979.

Harper, Brad, and Paul Metzger. *Exploring Ecclesiology: An Evangelical and Ecumenical Introduction*. Grand Rapids: Brazos, 2009.

Hilotin, Jay. "Deadly Scroll Without End: How Infinite Scroll Hacks Your Brain and Why It Is Bad for You." *Gulf News*, Feb. 21, 2023. https://gulfnews.com/amp/special-reports/deadly-scroll-without-end-how-infinite-scroll-hacks-your-brain-and-why-it-is-bad-for-you-1.1676965239566.

Holman, Colin. "Luther: The Musician." *Christianity Today*, Mar. 6, 2018. https://www.christianitytoday.com/history/2018/march/martin-luther-musician.html.

Holocaust Encyclopedia. "Dietrich Bonhoeffer." United States Holocaust Memorial Museum. https://encyclopedia.ushmm.org/content/en/article/dietrich-bonhoeffer.

Howarth, Josh. "Alarming Average Screen Time Statistics." Exploding Topics, June 24, 2024. https://explodingtopics.com/blog/screen-time-stats.

James, Samuel D. "Is Google Making Us Ungodly?" Crossway, Oct. 29, 2023. https://www.crossway.org/articles/is-google-making-us-ungodly/.

Jefferson, Robin Seaton. "Remembering the Rev. Billy Graham and How He Led an Older Generation's America from the Pulpit." *Forbes*, Feb. 21, 2018. https://www.forbes.com/sites/robinseatonjefferson/2018/02/21/remembering-the-rev-billy-graham-and-how-he-led-an-older-generations-america-from-the-pulpit/.

Jones, Owen. "Politicians Are Right About the 'Decline of the West'—But So Wrong About the Causes." *The Guardian*, Apr. 5, 2023. https://www.theguardian.com/commentisfree/2023/apr/05/decline-of-the-west-causes-moral-decay-living-standards.

Keener, Craig S. "Pentecostal Biblical Interpretation/Spirit Hermeneutics." In *Scripture and Its Interpretation: A Global, Ecumenical Introduction to the Bible*, edited by Michael J. Gorman, 270–83. Grand Rapids: Baker Academic, 2017.

Kempis, Thomas à. *The Imitation of Christ*. Translated by Ronald Knox and Michael Oakley. San Francisco: Ignatius, 2005.

Lewis, C. S. *The Lion, the Witch and the Wardrobe*. London: HarperCollins, 2009.

Lindsley, Arthur W. "C. S. Lewis on Chronological Snobbery." C. S. Lewis Institute, Mar. 5, 2003. https://www.cslewisinstitute.org/resources/c-s-lewis-on-chronological-snobbery/.

Mackie, Tim, et al. "Literature for a Lifetime." *BibleProject Podcast*, The Paradigm series, episode 6. Oct. 18, 2021.

Mbiti, John S. *African Religions and Philosophy*. 2nd ed. Portsmouth, NH: Heinemann, 1990.

Metaxas, Eric. *Bonhoeffer: Pastor, Martyr, Prophet, Spy*. Nashville: Nelson, 2020.

Bibliography

Morris, Henry M. "The Uttermost Parts of the Earth." Institute for Creation Research, Mar. 4, 2011. https://www.icr.org/article/uttermost-parts-earth.

Oral Roberts University. "Vision and Mission." https://oru.edu/about-oru/vision-and-mission/.

Packer, J. I. "Overview of Lectio Divina." C. S. Lewis Institute. https://www.cslewisinstitute.org/resources/overview-of-lectio-divina/.

Pew Research Center. "Frequency of Reading Scripture Among Christians." 2014. https://www.pewresearch.org/religious-landscape-study/database/christians/christian/frequency-of-reading-scripture/.

Ponder, Lindsey. "Literature for a Lifetime Show Notes." *BibleProject Podcast*, The Paradigm series, episode 6. Oct. 18, 2021. https://bibleproject.com/podcast/literature-lifetime/.

Price, Cory. "How Many Countries Are There in the World?" WorldAtlas, May 18, 2023. https://www.worldatlas.com/geography/how-many-countries-are-there-in-the-world.html.

Price, Randall. "A Reminder to Remember." *Israel My Glory* (July/Aug. 2022). https://israelmyglory.org/article/a-reminder-to-remember/August 2022.

Ratcliffe, Susan, ed. "St. Augustine of Hippo AD 354–430: Roman Christian Theologian." In *Oxford Essential Quotations*. 5th ed. Oxford: Oxford University Press, 2017. https://www.oxfordreference.com/display/10.1093/acref/9780191843730.001.0001/q-oro-ed5-00000572?rskey=SW0ZZK&result=186.

Scazzero, Peter. *Emotionally Healthy Discipleship: Moving from Shallow Christianity to Deep Transformation*. Grand Rapids: Zondervan, 2021.

Shelley, Bruce. *Church History in Plain Language*. Nashville: Thomas Nelson, 2008.

Spurgeon, C. H. "Honey in the Mouth." In *The Metropolitan Tabernacle Pulpit: Sermons Preached by C. H. Spurgeon*, 37:373–84. London: Banner of Truth Trust, 1970.

Stott, John. "Culture and the Bible." InterVarsity, Dec. 16, 2023. https://ism.intervarsity.org/resource/culture-and-bible.

Sweet, Leonard, and Frank Viola. *Jesus Manifesto: Restoring the Supremacy and Sovereignty of Jesus Christ*. Nashville: Thomas Nelson, 2010.

Travis, Melissa Cain. *Thinking God's Thoughts: Johannes Kepler and the Miracle of Cosmic Comprehensibility*. Moscow, ID: Roman Roads, 2022.

United States Holocaust Museum. "Weimar Germany Reichsbanknote, 50 million mark." Joel Forman Collection. https://collections.ushmm.org/search/catalog/irn524937.

Wesley, John. "Light Yourself on Fire with Passion and People Will Come from Miles to Watch You Burn." Goodreads. https://www.goodreads.com/quotes/626960-light-yourself-on-fire-with-passion-and-people-will-come.

Willard, Dallas. "Spiritual Formation in Christ Is for the Whole Life and Whole Person." In *For All the Saints: Evangelical Theology and Christian Spirituality*, edited by Timothy George and Alister McGrath, 39–53.

Bibliography

Louisville: Westminster John Knox, 2003. https://conversatio.org/spiritual-formation-in-christ-is-for-the-whole-life-and-the-whole-person/.

Wilson, Jared C. "Why Narnia Isn't Allegorical." The Gospel Coalition, Feb. 23, 2017. https://www.thegospelcoalition.org/article/why-narnia-isnt-allegorical/.

www.ingramcontent.com/pod-product-compliance
Lightning Source LLC
Chambersburg PA
CBHW060413090426
42734CB00011B/2300